The Art of
RAYMOND JONSON
Painter

Photograph by Henry Clark, 1944.

The Art of
RAYMOND JONSON
Painter

Ed Garman

Foreword by Elaine de Kooning

UNIVERSITY OF NEW MEXICO PRESS

Albuquerque

© 1976 by the University of New Mexico Press. All rights reserved
Library of Congress Catalog Card Number 75-21185
International Standard Book Number 0-8263-0404-4
Manufactured in the United States of America
First Edition

Composed by the University of New Mexico Printing Plant.
Printed and bound by North Central Publishing Co.
Designed by Dan Stouffer.

To Vera Jonson
companion in creativity

The Beautiful . . . were never in the Matter, but in the Art and Design; never in body itself, but in the Form or forming Power. Does not the beautiful Form confess this, and speak the Beauty of the Design, whene'er it strikes you? What is it but the Design which strikes?

Anthony Ashley Cooper
Third Earl of Shaftesbury
(1671–1713)

Contents

Illustrations

Photographs of Raymond Jonson

Frontispiece: Jonson, 1944, by Henry Clark

Following page 168:
    Jonson, 1914, by Eugene Hutchinson
    Jonson, 1962, by Helge Gilbert
    Jonson, 1966, by John Waggaman
    Jonson, 1975, by John Waggaman

Foreword

Raymond Jonson, at last, receives a fitting analysis and tribute in this valuable book by a fellow artist, Ed Garman. One is tempted to say that any analysis of Jonson and his work would inevitably tend to become a tribute.

If Jonson had continued to live and work in Chicago, where he began his career as an artist, or in New York, he would now have a national reputation. As it is, although he is represented in some fifty museums and public collections, his work has never been given a major showing and is therefore more or less unknown outside a small circle of knowledgeable admirers.

Jonson was twenty-two years old at the time of the 1913 Armory Show in Chicago, a crucial experience for the already strongly motivated young painter. Kandinsky's *The Art of Spiritual Harmony*, which he read about that time, also had a profound influence on his direction as an artist. In 1917 he had his first one-man show. In 1918 he made his first sale to a museum. In the twenties and thirties he exhibited regularly in Chicago and New York, but a fateful decision in 1922 to build a house in Santa Fe finally led to his disappearing into "the land of enchantment," New Mexico, there to turn out a tremendous number of paintings through years of rigorous daily work, a discipline the invincibly young eighty-four-year-old artist still follows. It was, for Jonson, a simple matter of choosing between a career and a vocation.

I heard of Raymond Jonson before I met him, and, I might say, I sensed his presence before I heard of him.

Shortly after my first visit to Albuquerque to teach at the University of New Mexico in 1957, I began to meet, one after the other, a number of dedicated young abstract artists working on their own in various directions but animated, it seemed, with a kind of communal energy and sense of purpose, and a notably high level of awareness of current avant garde trends in painting. There were about twelve of them in the city—something of a phenomenon in a population of 200,000. Albuquerque is not an artists' colony like Santa Fe or Taos, where, among hundreds of artists, it is logical to find a few serious ones who escape the deadly provinciality of artists' colonies in general. There's nothing provincial about Albuquerque—bleak, impersonal, uningratiating, a big-city-in-the-making with little time for art. When there is no response, artists tend to lose their impetus and concentration or to become eccentrics, doggedly working away in blind alleys, disconnected from the main thoroughfares. These artists, however, were thriving, not financially, but in the quality of their consciousness. I was curious about their buoyant resistance to neglect. Discussing the disastrous effects of indifference, one of these painters said to me, "The brush would have dropped from my hand if it hadn't been for Raymond Jonson." She explained that they all had studied with Jonson at the University of New Mexico some ten years earlier and that since then he had been giving them shows at his gallery. Hardly anyone came to the shows except the other artists and friends; still, a show was an incentive and there was, after all, that one pair of eyes whose response was worth working for. When I met Jonson, I knew I had found the key—the force that created a climate that enabled art to endure in a desert.

Jonson's presence is magical. Wise, quick-witted, merry, with amazing light-filled eyes and fantastic silver eyebrows that flash away like tumbleweeds across a super highway, he exudes an unearthly vitality. It is impossible to think of Jonson as separate from his painting. He lives, literally, in the center of a lifetime's work. In 1947, the University of New Mexico erected a building for Jonson to use as studio, living quarters, storage space, and a gallery to exhibit his own work and that of other artists. If other universities and public institutions throughout the country followed this magnificent gesture, it would do much to relieve the shocking neglect of living American artists, largely ignored by the powerful PR mechanism that treats art as merchandise and/or entertainment. At this point, the University of New Mexico's Jonson Gallery owns 670 works by Jonson (the gallery also owns a growing collection of some five hundred works by other artists). Beginning with 1918, every year of Jonson's life as an artist is represented in the gallery by at least one example of his work—offering a unique opportunity to study the evolution of an artist over a span of more than sixty years.

The impact of this accumulated work is overwhelming. Small, intense, hypnotic, Jonson's paintings are characterized by an almost fanatical precision and control. To the discipline of immaculate craftsmanship and a highly formulated imagery, he brings a paradoxical sense of emotional commitment almost mystical in effect. Although his painting varies in method, attitude, and form through the years, there is always an underlying singleness of purpose. In a catalog for a retrospective exhibition of Jonson's work in 1964, Ed Garman wrote:

> The manifestations of growth in this artist are as logical as the varied elements of root and stem, leaf, flower and fruit are logical to a single plant. There is a consistency of intention in his art. It is essentially an emotional quality which relates to his character. There is also a consistency of style, regardless of idea or process. Concepts may differ, the visual perspective may be varied, but his paintings are essentially of one character despite a diversity that at times seems otherwise. . . . The paintings themselves have a singing quality about them, a subtle sound, a pitch, a tonal mood that is characteristic even in the most brilliant contrasts, the strongest arrangements of line and shape, space and mass. There is a glowing freshness and a poise; a peace-giving serenity that is musically on rest.

Ed Garman, a California painter who met Jonson in 1938, writes from thirty-seven years' intimate knowledge of Jonson's paintings and ideas based on numerous conversations and extensive research in pertinent journals, letters, and records. All of this material is brilliantly organized to present an extraordinary evocation of Jonson's life, his philosophy, and his work. A rare and reverent book about a rare and reverent artist.

ELAINE DE KOONING

Plate 1. *Violet Light (The Artist's Wife Vera).* 1918. Oil, 44x33 inches.

Plate 2. *Symphonic Portrait—May Van Dyke*. 1929. Oil, 70x50 inches.

Plate 3. *Abstraction in Red.* 1932. Oil, 24x20 inches.

Plate 4. *Prismatic Figuration*. 1934. Oil, 20x15 inches.

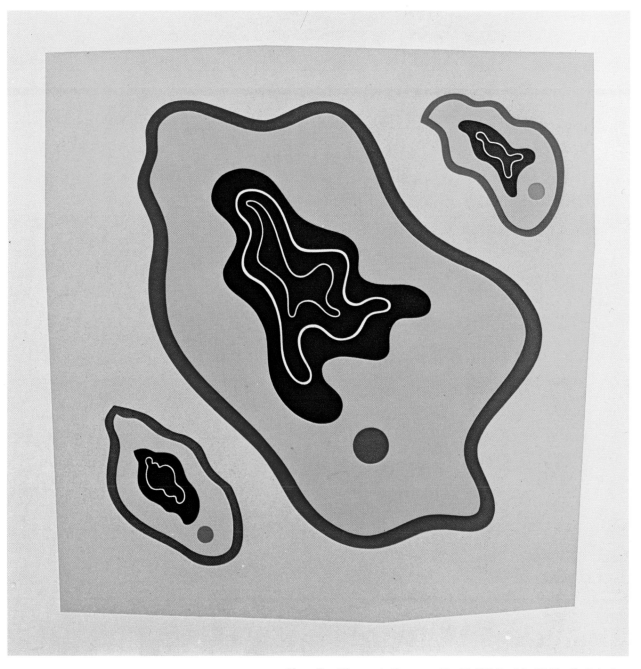

Plate 5. *Chromatic Contrasts No. 21 (Oil No. 11—1946).* 40x40 inches.

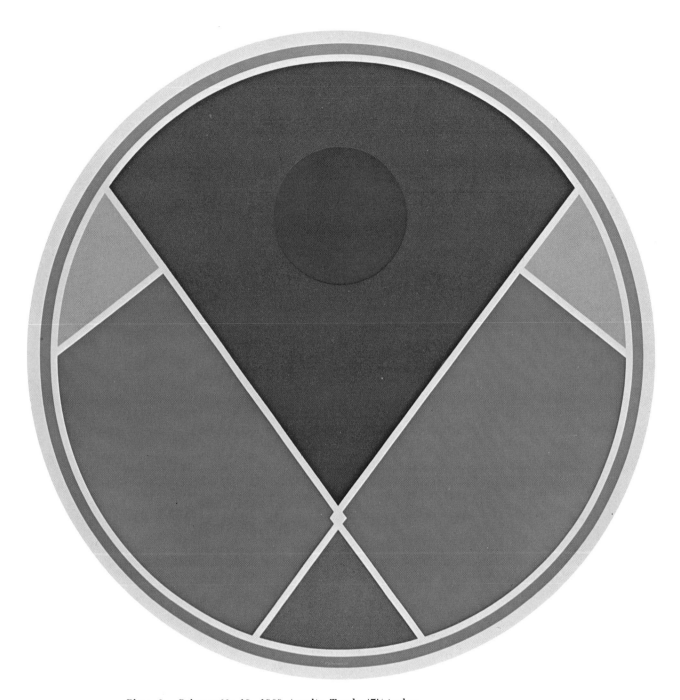

Plate 6. *Polymer No. 19—1969*. Acrylic, Tondo 47¼ inches.

Plate 7. *Polymer No. 4—1973*. Acrylic, 39x48 inches.

Plate 8. *Polymer No. 24–1973.* Four cutout open spatial
shapes. Acrylic, 42x33 inches. See also Figure 69.

Preface

In writing about the art of Raymond Jonson (pronounced "Jōnson"), the focus of attention has been on the work rather than on biographical minutiae. Consequently I have, to a large extent, limited biographical details to those events which directly affected his work, and an effort has been made to tie such information to the progressive stages of his evolution as an artist. Jonson himself has been cooperative, opening his files to me and joining in consultations to clarify his ideas and procedures.

Because the Jonson Reserved Retrospective Collection–The University of New Mexico contains typical examples of the artist's work from each year of his production, beginning with 1912, this study has been based almost entirely on it. With the exception of *Light* (Figure 11) and of *Composition Four—Melancholia* (Figure 16), together with two pencil drawings from Jonson's diaries (Figures 12 and 14), all of the works reproduced herein are in that collection. Therefore, it has seemed unnecessary to give this information on each of the reproductions. Where dimensions of works are mentioned they are in inches with height preceding width.

For those interested in more biographical details or information as to the location of other works a chronology and a list of public institutions owning Jonson works have been added following the text.

The author wishes to extend his appreciation to Roland Dickey, who gave important criticism in the early phases of the book's development. To Arthur Johnson gratitude is due for the time and knowledge he has contributed in reading and criticizing the manuscript. It was he who typed the manuscript in its final form and who supplied the supplementary sections of Chronology, Public Collections, Notes, and Index.

A very special word of praise is due to John Waggaman for his exemplary photographs of Jonson's works. Although not specifically noted on each reproduction, all of them, with the exception of Figures 5 and 12 by Thomas E. Zudick, Figure 11 by Ken Cobean, and Figures 16, 21, and 33, the photographers of which are unknown, are from photographs by Mr. Waggaman.

Financial assistance in the publication of the book has been afforded by the Jonson Gallery–UNM Publications Fund. This fund was generously established by Charles Morris and was subsequently the beneficiary of gifts from Mrs. B. J. O. Nordfeldt (Emily), Norman and Vighi Allen, Gene and Eunice Calkins, Carl Edge, Jerry and Florence Chakerian, James L. and Julia La Fon, Mrs. Grace Tharp, Frank and Evelyn Walker, Sam and Mae Green (Maera), Harold and Catherine Fisher, George and Helene Simson, Sam and Jane Rankin, Lawrence and Lanette Wilkinson, Morris and Alyce Haas, and Carsten and Maude Steffens.

The author and publisher acknowledge with gratitude indebtedness for brief quotations in the text to Dell Publishing Company for Sam Hunter's *Modern American Painting and Sculpture;* to Farrar & Rinehart for Floyd Dell's *Homecoming: An Autobiography;* to the Macmillan Company for Alfred North Whitehead's *Science and the Modern World;* to the Munson-Williams-Proctor Institute for a passage from *1913 Armory Show 50th Anniversary Exhibition Catalog, 1963;* to Simon & Schuster for Thomas Craven's *Men of Art;* to Frederick A. Stokes Co., for Clive Bell's *Art;* to University of California Press for Frederick S. Wight's *Arthur G. Dove;* to University of Indiana Press and Victor Gollancz, London, for Maurice Browne's *Too Late to Lament;* to Wittenborg, Schultz for Louis H. Sullivan's *Kindergarten Chats;* and to the following magazines: *Art in America* for quotations from Elaine de Kooning; *Art News* for a statement by Lawrence Campbell; *Arts Magazine* for comments by Alfred Werner; *El Palacio* for a quotation from Frederick O'Hara; *New Mexico Magazine* for an excerpt from Ina Sizer Cassidy; *Poetry: A Magazine of Verse* for a note by Harriet Monroe; and *Theatre Arts Magazine* for quotations from Raymond Jonson and Eunice Tietjens.

Finally, there are the many others who have contributed in one way or another to the realization of the book. My thanks go to my patient wife Coreva, to the editors and publisher, and particularly to Elaine de Kooning, who, in the midst of her very busy life, took the time to write her lively foreword.

Prologue

1912 November: "To conceive an idea and work on this idea, not to convert it into something physical but to express just the idea shorn of all superfluous materialism—would it not be a piece of expression?"

1918 November: "Won't paint as a color and material, if properly used, if the mind sees light, do what nothing else can do—create the spirit of emotion that is felt and therefore created by the creator?"

1921 April: "The work for itself, to stand as the expression of an emotion, the abstract, spiritual ego of the individual."

1938 January: "Art's office is the creation of a unity. It is concerned in bringing about the fusion of matter with spirit, which is the object of creation itself."

1949 October: "As order is parallel with quality we find in the absolute idiom a means to establish it in the highest degree known to date. And because the material making up the concept comes from the inner rather than the outer, I believe a closer approach to the spiritual is possible."[1]

1

Introduction

The foregoing quotations introduce thoughts and ideals the painter Raymond Jonson expressed, and they indicate the direction his art has followed throughout his life. Once more in 1971 he confirmed his point of view when he wrote:

> My aim has been to present original concepts based on a solid technical foundation and arriving at a high degree of paint quality, clarity of statement of the particular design or structure, with an aliveness, and when possible, a dynamic impact and feeling of over-all rightness through craftsmanship. My hope has been that through the intuitive or subconscious act a feeling of the spiritual, rather than the physical, would occur at times.[1]

The consistency of Jonson's effort to achieve his expressed aims has made him meaningful to others as an example of single-minded devotion to an ideal. To those who know him through his art, his name stands for painting with high integrity. To those who know him as a person, he stands for a particular way of life. It is a way that has brought satisfactions to Jonson in that he has felt that it has been lived in a constructive atmosphere.

Raymond Jonson has been described as "a one-man task force for modern art in New Mexico,"[2] and again as "a powerful counterforce to provincialism."[3] It should be kept in mind that for many years he was close to being an isolated figure among New Mexico painters. Visiting artists made little contribution to the cause of modern art insofar as bringing understanding to the people of New Mexico was concerned. Jonson, however, was always making propaganda for the modern point of view.[4]

Because he has lived and worked in New Mexico for fifty of his eighty-four years, he is better known in the Southwest than elsewhere even though public and private collections from coast to coast contain his works.

After a decade and a half of studying and painting in Chicago, Jonson settled at Santa Fe in 1924. There he became the "Modernist" member of its art colony.[5] In Santa Fe and later in Albuquerque, as he had in Chicago, he devoted his life not only to the creative aspects of art but also to activities which have invigorated interest in and appreciation of modern art by those about him.

In 1934 Jonson began teaching at the University of New Mexico in Albuquerque as a part-time instructor. When he retired from teaching at the university some twenty years later, it was as a full professor. By that time his battle to gain recognition in New Mexico for modern art as a full-fledged member of the family of arts, a battle which as time passed had brought many allies to his side, had been won.

Jonson's view of what art should be, how the arts should function, and particularly his concern about the preservation and care of works of art were things he wished to share with others. Nor were his ideas on such subjects related only to his own work. He felt that the activities embodied in the creation and showing of works of art have important values for individual and community life. In Santa Fe, as the art colony expanded to include other painters with a contemporary viewpoint, he had, as a kind of unofficial curator for modern art at the Museum of New Mexico, arranged for a "Modern Wing" (1927–31) in which he mounted monthly exhibitions of works by the group of eligible artists. Similarly out of his beliefs and ideals there grew the idea of the project for the Jonson Gallery–The University of New Mexico (Figures 1 and 2), which was formally opened to the public in January of 1950.

The idea of the gallery and its collections was conceived and developed into a coherent plan by 1947. Because of his long and happy association with the university Jonson hoped that his work would remain there permanently, that the university would become the custodian of his life effort, so that a substantial and substantive collection of the works produced in a spirit of idealism would become public rather than private property. At that time

Figure 1.   Jonson Gallery–The University of New Mexico.

Figure 2.   Jonson Gallery–The University of New Mexico.
Interior showing a corner of the gallery.

the university was without a museum or art collection so, with his private collection as a nucleus, he hoped also to establish a representative collection of works by other artists.

The university accepted Jonson's plan early in 1948. It then took two years to achieve its physical realization. The university provided a campus site for the building and established the gallery's status as an intrinsic segment of the university, an autonomous unit within the university's College of Fine Arts.[6]

In undertaking the financial and supervisory responsibilities involved in carrying out the project from the ground up, Jonson and his wife Vera put all they possessed into it. Even so the plan might have foundered had it not been for gifts from donors who believed in the validity of Jonson's idea, particularly the gifts of Frank C. Rand, Jr. and Adele Levis Rand, which were decisive in making the project financially feasible.[7]

When the gallery opened with a retrospective exhibition of Jonson's work, the artist was able to announce the concurrent establishment of several permanent collections including not only his own work but that of other artists.[8] Of primary importance is the Jonson Reserved Retrospective Collection, which contains representative examples from each of the years of the artist's career. It involves a full survey of his work with examples of each type, all the various techniques he has employed, and all the mediums he has used. It provides the unique opportunity to study the evolution of an artist over a span of more than sixty years through a definitive collection in one place.

The care and preservation of his own and other artists' works were not the sole objectives. The gallery's functions have included the expanding of Jonson's contact with the public, the provision of a testing ground for himself and other exploratory artists, the affording to artists, particularly young artists, a place in which to exhibit their work. Often these were the first one-man exhibitions by these artists.[9]

Beyond these objectives Jonson felt there were implications of a wider nature, for he said at the time of the formal opening:

Because of this gift and the gifts of others who have joined with me I am aligning with them in believing all this will stimulate widespread interest and will encourage contributions by others toward this and other cultural activities. My interest is in art.

Therefore I insist that the entire effort be considered one of presenting to the people a symbol of creative living. . . . If, through the demonstration I hope to carry out, some light can be thrown upon the problems of the artist, especially for our students, it may be an incentive for greater faith and work. If I can . . . contribute in various ways to an environment that has as its basis that of the spirit rather than the physical all the agony, sacrifice and work will not have been in vain.[10]

In the examination of the evolution of Jonson's art as fully exemplified in the Retrospective Collection we realize that the complex of growth and change in expression from the earliest of his works to the latest will, of necessity, require observations from a variety of viewpoints. The development of his work shows an intricate pattern, a diversity, that will call for the unraveling of its threads with patience if we are to understand what his art means and what his contributions to art have been.

To submit Jonson's course to a simple calendar chronology would be both inaccurate and deceptive. There are a number of things in the chronicle of Jonson's art which, like nature's biological clocks, run at different rates. It should be noted that of the several things to be seen in the development of his art, one is a peculiar directionless act of achieving a direction. Early in his career he wrote, "the usual tendency is to find a path and stick to it. I say travel that path but gather all that grows along its side."[11]

It is clear that, although there are several powerful lines of direction, they were not held to in the degree that would exclude the enjoyment of any digression, however irrelevant to the main direction it might seem to be. Jonson felt sure of his direction. Whatever the detour, he could resume the primary path, bringing to it whatever enrichment the diversion may have supplied.

The thoughts recorded in his letters and diaries were not always simultaneously reflected in his work. Although he was in general accord with the main directions of modern art, most of the time he was out of synchronization with it. He did not leap into the painting of abstraction or nonobjective works even though in his diary, at an early date, he was writing about such things. Nor was he then interested in the development of a formal philosophy of art. His fundamental ideas emerged early but were often submerged by the immediate day-to-day problems of painting and expression to reemerge perhaps as much as a decade later. In the development of his works there was a distinct lag between expectation and accomplishment. The sincerity of his temperament forced him to move slowly and cautiously. His prime consideration was that his growth should be an organic one dependent on self-integration, rather than a bold attack on the frontiers of painting and its esthetics. Even more, he had a reluctance to accept the developments in art vicariously or accept any new movement as a matter of faith.

His assimilation of influences is another example of a fractured chronology. Whether from nature, books, paintings, works of art in other areas, or other artists, an idea received at one point in time might not surface until years later when the source was forgotten. This mulling and integrating give a partial explanation for the obscurity of influences in his work.

There was an imperious demand for experience of the manifold means available to the artist. Whatever might be transpiring in other studios, he felt a compulsion to express the potentialities of whatever phenomena aroused him. Could he honestly "attempt to create abstract forms"[12] when he had not sufficiently exploited the possibilities in the "forms of nature?"[13] Consequently, he took no shortcuts, nor did he move directly into abstraction. At every stage of his development as an artist he has come to the next step simply because he has utilized for himself the potentialities of the previous step. Something in his makeup as a man and an artist forbade the acceptance of the experiments and experiences of others as sufficient; he must himself live and work through each phase. As a result, he has never been of any school but has gone his personal way, and at no time has he adopted the ideas, methods, or mannerisms of the various groups that have achieved prominence during his lifetime. Although he has been in the forefront of modernism, he has not made being a "modernist" his objective. He was primarily an individualistic artist conscious of and submitting to the evolutionary process taking place in his work.

2

Beginnings

Raymond Jonson was born on 18 July 1891 on the farm of his maternal grandparents, immigrant Swedish farmers who had settled in Lucas County, Iowa, shortly after the end of the Civil War. Carl Abrahamson, the grandfather, was a Baptist and so, also, was Jonson's father. The absence of a vested human spiritual authority was fundamental to their belief. One may safely hazard that this spiritual individualism, which permeated the atmosphere of his boyhood, was a main source of the faith in artistic individualism that would become a central factor in Jonson's life as an artist.

American history tells us that the half-century from 1860 to 1910 included the great migrations of people from all over the world to America seeking to realize what they could of the "American Dream." It was a period of expanding horizons, the exploitation of frontiers, the individual facing his problems and his future. Self-awareness and self-reliance were like passwords to that future. There was a spirit of optimism and expectation which nothing, neither wars nor stock market panics, nor labor unrest, which indeed were symptoms of the times, could dampen. A philosopher like Ralph Waldo Emerson, who distilled thought from living Americans themselves, proclaimed the spirit of the era in essays that summoned the nation to intellectual freedom, to self-trust and self-reliance, and to the genius that is the awareness of, the importance of, and the dignity of the individual man who trusts his instincts and acts on them.

To Americans, native born and immigrants alike, this was their birthright: to be free, individualistic, true to themselves. Jonson's parents, both European born, lived in this social and philosophical atmosphere even though they might not have known of Emerson or been able to express that which was basic to their lives. They were no longer European, but aggressively American. Nor is it unreasonable to suppose that such concepts were, at least subconsciously, formative influences on Jonson's thoughts and ideals; for he was to express himself in similar terms in later years.

As a boy he followed his minister father from Iowa to Minnesota, Wyoming, Colorado, Kansas, and finally to Oregon. The family moved from one church parish to the next, living a rootless life so that the father might preach. There were countless sermons and prayer meetings to attend, months and years of a life with little cash, much sacrifice, and hard work. It was the sort of life that put one on one's own resources, that taught self-discipline and dedication to purpose. It built a type of integrity that would enable a man to go the whole way alone, should such be the necessity, once he had found his dedication.

In 1902 the family arrived in Portland, Oregon, a place in which it could take root and stay. Here Jonson grew up and went to school, and here he had his first introduction to art instruction.

In a letter to the author, Raymond's brother Arthur has given this picture of their beginnings:

> Father rented a house, bought furniture and dishes and *an oil painting.* . . . It belonged to the Hudson River school, more or less. . . . It was a painting in a tremendous gold frame—a huge thing that followed us from house to house.
>
> I want you to try to imagine the situation—here is a man of God, his promised salary is minuscule, he has six children, the eldest around 11, in a new world . . . and in all the worry and trouble and penny-pinching of getting a start, a veritable original work of art was apparently considered an appropriate object to acquire.

In the same letter there are further insights into Jonson's youth:

> Item two in the catalog of basic character-forming circumstances is that of money. We never had any. We were poor but

proud—even proud of it. At least I was. This weird pride in being poor is one of my strangest memories of my boyhood. . . . Raymond, too, must have gone through some comparable experience because he has rarely resented the lack of money except when, in specific instances, it has interfered with his work. We all knew from the outset that we were on our own financially. . . . When Raymond pulled up and went to Chicago he went on his own money—how he had worked for it and how he had hoarded it. Even so he'd undoubtedly paid "board and room" at home as we all did whenever we made any money. . . . I'm not sure at just what age he had decided to be an artist but he had made the decision before he knew that there really were people who were just that and nothing but that. I remember his excited study of pictures in magazines, real hand-drawn pictures and in his earliest teens he was making judgements as to which were good and which were not. I remember him, when I was 6 or 7, exclaiming in much the same style that I heard from him 20 or so years later over a drawing that pleased him.[1]

An important source of income for young Jonson was as a paper carrier for the *Oregonian,* the *Journal,* and the *Telegram,* part of the time for all three simultaneously. He soon became acquainted with the people and skills involved in the production of the papers. One of these skills, that of the pictorial commentator, the editorial cartoonist, interested the boy. It was this phase of drawing that first excited him.

In 1909 the Portland Art Association established its Museum Art School, and Jonson was its first enrolled student. His instructor, Kate Cameron Simmons, had studied at the Pratt Institute in Brooklyn under Arthur Wesley Dow, among whose notable students were Georgia O'Keeffe, Agnes Pelton, and Max Weber. "Dow was one of the pioneers of the new interest in Oriental art, and he had been at Pont-Aven with Gauguin and Emile Bernard. His interest in the decorative styles of Japanese art and in a non-naturalistic use of color, as exemplified by Gauguin and the Nabis, made him an enlightened and vital teacher."[2]

In his teaching, "Dow was strongly against the storytellers and those who believed that close imitation of nature was the primary reason for a work of art. Dow taught the non-naturalistic use of color and brought

Japanese prints into his class, teaching space relations and the proper balance of light and dark masses—in short, plastic design. He emphasized structure, spirit, imagination—creation."[3]

One may speculate as to how much of Dow's modern spirit and teaching Kate Simmons brought to her classroom, or as to the depth and duration of the influence on Jonson. Such speculation suggests that, perhaps unknowingly, he had received preparation both for resistance to the academic and commercial viewpoint to which he was later exposed, and for response, in a spirit akin to Dow's, to the modern and progressive attitudes when he encountered them.

In its first year the Portland Museum Art School course of study included Sketch Class, General Drawing, Color, and Elementary Design, the last described in the catalog as "The principles of constructive and decorative art, with application in original problems of space and line composition, in tones and in color."[4]

This contact with drawing from the model and a simple sort of approach to composition produced in him the urge to enroll in a full-time course on a more comprehensive scale than was then possible in Portland. He decided that he would go to Chicago for study at the Chicago Academy of Fine Arts, prompted to this decision by his friend Victor Vance who had studied there. The Academy was essentially a commercial school, one of the best of its type, engaged in turning out professional people capable of producing art work on demand. The school was thoroughly academic and did an excellent job in its field. To it, as a student, Jonson brought an intense desire and eagerness to learn. Six days after his arrival in Chicago he was enrolled at the Academy.

3

Sense of Mission

Jonson was a person with a sense of mission. His attitude toward his mission was not that of a practical person who had found a role in life and had the common sense to live it. With him there was a mystical side to it. His mental attitude might be summed up by the old maxim that miracles come to those whose minds are prepared for them. Again to quote from Arthur:

> No one can know Raymond for long and not feel the impact that religion—and I use the word in its broadest possible meaning—has had on his character and life. Indeed, without stretching the meaning of words too much, one could say his whole life has been a religious activity.
>
> The foundation is the hard rock of the Baptist faith of our parents. If you know anything about Baptist doctrines you know that to them religion comes as an individual, personal "experience." Many are called but few are chosen. Raymond was both called and chosen. . . . The whole mystical background of religion is part of Raymond's background. The "experience" is something he has known. It has affected his work.[1]

In August 1949, in a paper prepared for and read to the Chili Club of Santa Fe, Jonson recounted some of the spiritual experiences that had shaped his life. The first two of these follow:

> Portland, Oregon, 1902. Without warning while alone one day in our home, when I was about eleven years old, I had the feeling

that God in person appeared to me and informed me I was ready to be converted to Jesus and join the church. I was convinced and experienced what I suppose was an hour or so of religious ecstasy. When the family returned I tried to explain what had happened but they considered me too young to know these things. But I insisted I knew and there was only one thing to do—immediately baptize me into the church. I succeeded in this. But the church failed me. Some eight or nine years later I realized the particular church was narrow-minded, bigoted and hypocritical to such an extent I turned against it in disgust. Realize I now am saying I turned against that church, not my original experience.

Chicago, 1911. Sometime after I left home and set out for further art training I had another spiritual experience—this time pertaining to art. As a result I came to the conclusion that my life was to be dedicated to art. How this was to be accomplished I had not the slightest idea, but I knew it had to be and that in time all would work out. During the next few years a radical change in my whole life took place and I came through it a different individual. From that time on it has been a constant aim to develop and create independently and honestly.[2]

4

The Chicago Academy
of Fine Arts

When Jonson arrived in Chicago in September of 1910 his intention was a commercial profession and its rewards. But very soon the immovable object of practicality had to reckon with the irresistible force of a genuine art spirit.

In the beginning Jonson, in an unsophisticated way, differentiated but slightly between fine art and commercial art. After only a few months at the Academy, he declared in his letters home that "cartooning and dead stiff commercial work is cheap art." He set his sights a little higher. "I am studying illustration now."[1] That too was threatened after a few visits to the exhibitions at the Art Institute. He wrote, "The Art Institute is a dream being dreamed while awake. It creates inspirations to go there. Oh, if only I had words to express the artistic feelings I get sometimes. Bet I will someday but on canvas I hope."[2]

The change from a conscientious attempt to become an illustrator to that of an inspired devotee of the fine arts was an exciting one. As we have seen, he saw it as a spiritual experience. Excerpts from his letters home show the excitement of his early school life and the charged feelings of his change:

> September 9, 1910. School is O.K. Am quite pleased with it. It means business and so do the students. . . . Everything has gone all right so far and it's going to continue.

> September 17. School is great—awfully interesting. . . . I was at the Art Institute this P.M. and it was wonderful—great. Hardly over it yet.

October 8. Real art seems the only thing now. . . . I went over to the Institute, only two blocks from school, and inquired concerning night classes. You see I'd like to take some study there too. . . . I want illustration and in oils if I can get it. . . . If I'm going to use color I believe it will help if I get it as I go along. Color is the art medium. One needs to study all the time.

November 25. Tell Papa his boy, if he ever amounts to anything, will not be a cartoonist but an artist. . . . Art, real art, for me.

December 11. School is wonderful. It's funny that I hadn't realized before how awfully much there is to learn. Not only art but to be an artist one should know an awful lot. I hope to; that's what makes it so great.

January 26, 1911. Great doings at school. Monday I started painting in life class. I think I shall take charcoal life two nights a week at school, too. I am going Fridays only at the Institute—anatomy, studying the construction of the human figure. It's all great.

February 6. I am painting now.

February 23. At the Institute is the most wonderful exhibition by Sorolla. It's so wonderful and good that no one can express it. He has studied all his life, is about 48 years old, a Spaniard, and is considered one of the world's greatest living artists. . . .[3] I tell you one certainly sees and learns much when so deeply interested (I might say in love) in that greatest study, Art.

March 5. Everything concerning school is O.K. except my ability to paint. (Rotten!) I refuse to discuss it.

March 16. I am well and plugging away hard as ever. . . . I hope to arrange so I'll have this summer to monkey around sketching and painting and studying.

May 14. School will be out in six weeks. Then watch me look around. I'm going to see this town then; the picture galleries especially.

October 18. School, of course is wonderful. If one only could do justice to oneself it would be all right. The opportunity is great so the best one can do is work. Progress is slow. So it is in all great things. Sunday one of the boys and I went out in the country to paint. Wonderful. It sure is lovely here this time of the year—color —whew! Great. Orange, yellow, blue and red. We had a great time.

October 25. The composition class is great. A Mr. Olson Nordfeldt instructs and he is a painter.

Thus it was that in October of 1911 Jonson made his first contact with B. J. O. Nordfeldt, who came to the Academy to take, temporarily, a class in composition. Nordfeldt, only thirteen years Jonson's senior, was born in Sweden and emerged from the immigrant environment of Chicago at the age of nineteen to begin his study at the Art Institute. He went on to New York and then to Paris where he spent a month or two at the Académie Julien before going off on his own, aroused by the power of Manet, Gauguin, and Cézanne. He became intrigued by the wood-block technique and went to England to study the process. In 1903 he was in Sweden and by 1905 he had returned to Chicago where he vigorously began to develop his painting. By 1910 he had fused Whistlerian concepts with Fauve-like colors and was among the first of American artists to whom the term "Expressionist" could be applied.

Nordfeldt's effect on Jonson was immediate, heightening his idealism and sharpening his sense of self-criticism. In the same letter of 25 October 1911 which told of study under Nordfeldt, he went on to say:

Ah if I only could do justice to it all, if only to a part, but I can't. We're all so rotten that if art should take form and should see our work she would *die.*

On November 10, he wrote:

I don't know how I am making out at school. I seem to get pretty good marks, but I can't see it. I don't believe they count or denote one's ability. All one can do is work on—there's always hope.

In other letters his self-criticism continued:

December 1. My work at school disgusts me. It isn't what it ought to be—I don't think it is. I'm taking a rest now and shall try over again on Monday.

December 14. I am troubled with my work. I am not doing what I expect and expected. It is very hard on me. They say I'm getting "crabby," grouchy, you know. I hope not. I don't feel that way but I do feel sad at times.

I guess everything will be all right, though. Do you know I'm getting into it so deep, that is art, that it seems the only thing for me. So you can see what it means when I can't get what I want. I must work on, of course. Maybe I don't work hard enough. . . . Maybe I ought not take my study too seriously but I can't help it, it's natural. I am thankful that things are as they are and not worse.

I am having a great experience at any rate—it really is great.

February 21, 1912. I am on a different road than I was 18 months ago. It's painting now—real art. . . . I am under one of the best painters-instructors in the United States and I had better stick.

March 1. I will not give up till I've either reached the top or the rungs on the ladder above me break off. . . . So now life must take its course. I have big ambitions and high ideals but we can never strive too high.

April 21. There are two or three things I want to do eventually—paint and etch and draw, but I will do anything as a means to that end.

I came here to do cartooning. Two months killed it. . . . You know it's in our youth we are made or unmade. . . . I shall now make a statement. I will stick to the end, building a foundation. 'Way down I have a feeling that I want to do something different in art and if I ever find it I shall do it in spite of all. If the people or the world fail to recognize it, very well. I shall not desert it but shall take or pay the penalty.

Study—The Human Figure—Male (Figure 3) is a typical charcoal drawing from the academic classrooms of Jonson's school days. Done in 1912, it is a standard school pose and reveals the seriousness of purpose in

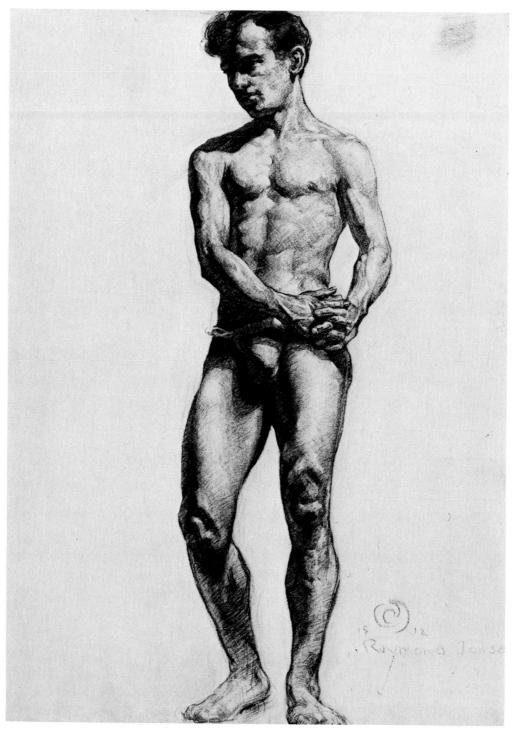

Figure 3. *Study—The Human Figure—Male.* 1912.
Charcoal, 23½x17½ inches.

Jonson as a student. It is one of the very few of his student studies to survive destruction and is now the earliest work in the Retrospective Collection.

Field Museum—Chicago (Figure 4) provides an example of Jonson's efforts in painting away from the classroom. The young student approached painting in oils with some apprehension. In addition to working in a class called "oil composition," he did a great deal of sketching from nature and some copying of paintings that seemed to include ingredients which, for one reason or another, had value for him. *Field Museum—Chicago* is reproduced here simply because it is the earliest Jonson painting in the Retrospective Collection and hence provides the point of departure for the artist's long journey in art. It was done outdoors, on his own, not as a class assignment. Its free brushing, its helter-skelter dash of color, celebrate a feeling for freshness and brightness.

Figure 4.   *Field Museum—Chicago.* 1912. Oil, 28x33 inches.

5

"The Little Studio"

At the age of twenty-one Jonson knew that paint was in his blood. He wrote to his family:

> Paint—ah, expression—paint. It's better than food and better than sleep. Well, it's the best I know of. How can one be sane and have the common conventional idea—"Get the money"—when he loves and is lost in the puddle of paint? How can one give up the best of life? One can leave his best ones, his loved ones, lose all earthly power and fame, but he cannot turn traitor to his palette. Color!! I'm afraid I love it too much.[1]

To the young Jonson the irresistible fascination of being lost in a puddle of paint was the call to his inevitable future. Painting offered freedom of choice for emotional action to a degree almost impossible in other disciplines. It gave the opportunity to work in a medium tolerant of paradoxes that allowed one to be as many different selves as one could wish. The problems were endless. One could set one's goal as wide and as high as one's imagination demanded and one's inner resources permitted. One could cast off authority, secede, and establish oneself as a congregation of one in worship of the true spirit. From his letters of the period we can feel his enthusiasm and dedication; we can tell from his unbounded ambition that he enjoyed every one of the possibilities that confronted him. It was characteristic that, having taken the first tentative steps, he would soon be rushing headlong. Once he had accepted this love, he was willing to endure any consequence so long as he could paint and make some progress in satisfying his need to discover, experience, and express. For all this he needed independence from the classroom and a place in which to enjoy his freedom and assert his individuality.

In May 1912 Jonson wrote to his parents, "I have a studio now. Three of us . . . from school have been planning on getting this place for a long time. At last we have it."[2]

The Chicago *Sunday Record-Herald* for 10 November 1912 carried an article entitled, "Chicago's Little Parnassus." It began, "Chicago has its own Quartier Latin," and explained:

> You go to Fifty-seventh street. . . . On either side of the street on which you stand is a row of what appear to be deserted store buildings, glass-fronted, one story in height, gingerbread work along the top . . . the stores run around in an L on either side of Fifty-seventh street to Stony Island avenue. About a dozen of the studios face inward upon Fifty-seventh street. The others, around the corner on Stony Island avenue, look across Jackson Park. . . .
>
> [There are] the dwellers in "The Little Studio," Sloan, Erickson and Jonson,[3] students who wouldn't be working half so hard, possibly, even in the artistic environment of all Paris, as they are doing in the Jackson Park art colony. . . .
>
> There's Nordfeldt. By right we should begin with Nordfeldt, eager, tense, critical, absorbed in perfecting his own genius, contemptuous of triflers, critical of contemporaries. He was one of the first, if not the first, to discover the studios as artistic possibilities. . . .[4]

This was the beginning of Jonson's sustained contact with B. J. O. Nordfeldt. In the letter with which he sent a copy of the newspaper article, Jonson wrote to his family:

> Believe me, there are great doings out here. . . . Nordie, as we call him, strikes me as the most prominent amongst us. He is Sloan's and my strongest influence. He is fine. . . . He is called a "Post Impressionist." We call it "Expressionism" and it seems to be the core of art.[5]

In a later statement to the author, Jonson went into more details concerning this important contact:

> We set up our studio and associated with Nordfeldt as much as we could. He was, of course, busy painting. We saw a great deal of Nordy. He would drop in on us often.
>
> One morning he came in. It was rather late in the morning. We were painting and we had a model. An old woman was posing for us. Nordy said, "I guess I'll stay here awhile and see what you boys are doing. I'll sit back here in the corner."
>
> He would say something like this: "The red you're putting on there doesn't go with the yellow, it's too light or it's too dark. Now what do you think? Try it and see if you think it's right." So I would try it. Then he would say, "It looks all wrong to me. Try it the other way and then see what you think." So the other would be tried.
>
> There would be this type of discussion, back and forth, trial and error.
>
> On another occasion he came by, probably the next day and he said, "I'm disappointed in what you are doing. Has anyone around here got some canvas, some brushes, some paint I could use and I'll show you how it's to be done." So we fixed him up and he went to work and he painted the old lady very spontaneously and very quickly and went home. I still have the painting.[6]
>
> I've forgotten how long that went on but it went on for quite some time. You must remember that I was completely in sympathy with what Nordy said. Nordy knew what he was talking about in every respect.
>
> His influence was a very strong thing. How good it was I don't know. The stimulation and the experience were good. This very naturally would bring one close to the person giving such stimulation and I felt it was wonderful to have such an association.[7]

6

Growth

One of the many things the student of art must learn is to find an identification with that part of the mainstream of art that is most suited to his nature.

Jonson's identification with the modern concept of art seemed to exist almost from his earliest student days. At that time modern art was hardly the broadly delineated body of ideas and effects that we have with us today, though painting itself had just gone over a great watershed in a proliferation of innovations and styles. Painting was beginning to move into a full role as a member of the modern movement in the arts.

The modern spirit proclaimed itself in Chicago well before the turn of the century, not in painting or sculpture but in architecture. Chicago architecture clearly shifted interest from the idea of "appearances" to the idea of "structure." Sullivan wrote, "[A tall building] must be every inch a proud and soaring thing, rising in sheer exultation that from bottom to top it is a unit without a single dissenting line. . . ." [1] It is unlikely that any of the reigning painters knew, understood, or could transpose into their paintings the profound implications of Chicago architecture exemplified by the work of Louis H. Sullivan or Frank Lloyd Wright. In painting the main infusion of Modernism was that of Impressionism. There is little evidence of much serious practice or experimentation among Chicago artists of the period in the type of Modernism burgeoning in Paris, Rome, and other art capitals of the world.

When Arthur Dove's exhibition opened in Chicago in the middle of March 1912 it caused an unusual stir. Discussions about abstractions raged in newspapers, periodicals, and the gathering places of Chicago artists. Harriet Monroe, founder of *Poetry: A Magazine of Verse,* a leader of the Chicago literary renaissance, was a working art critic who patiently tried to present the case for modern art. Miss Monroe, who had listened to Dove speak, wrote in the *Chicago Tribune,* "Modern minds, he thinks, are reaching out toward an art of pure color and form dissociated from 'representation.' "[2]

George Cram Cook of the *Chicago Evening Post* had looked at the paintings and listened seriously to Dove, and wrote with unusual understanding:

> —[This] work is the point of the wedge that is being driven into the future. This is the real creative impulse of our century.
> —That's the word—the self-significance of color and line—regardless of what the colors and lines represent, or whether they represent anything.
> —But tell me: is this new painting really trying, as some say, to be music, or is it painting trying to be more itself?
> —I should say it was painting trying to use its own elements—lines, masses, colors—with the same freedom from representativeness which exists in musical notes—and rhythms. . . .[3]

Jonson took an interest in the discussions about Dove. They brought a degree of clarification to his viewpoint. Consequently, when the Armory Show arrived in Chicago in 1913, accompanied as it was by the venomous comments of critics and established conservative artists, Jonson was able to make an assessment of its effects on him.

The Armory Show was open at the Chicago Art Institute from 24 March to 16 April.

> It consisted of most of the foreign section plus a selected representation of American works, which altogether totalled about 500 objects. Chicago was titillated by the advance publicity but, being also provincially defensive, it assumed a hostile "show me" attitude. However, innuendos about the immorality of some of the exhibits, which coincided with one of those periodic legislative

investigations of morality, added to free admission on certain days, was too much to withstand and attendance soared. The general excitement was abetted by a concerted effort on the part of the faculty of the Chicago Art Institute's art school to ridicule the show in the galleries and to inflame the student body to burn Matisse[4] and Brancusi in effigy, as well as Walter Pach, who was trying to explain modern art. The purported discovery of four toes on a Matisse nude[5] was enough to relegate the new art to oblivion, but nearly 200,000 people came to see the exhibition, and perhaps a few of them took it seriously.[6]

Jonson did take it seriously.[7] Excitedly, he wrote to his mother:

Today the big International exhibit opened with a reception. Of course I was there. And such an exhibit. You must have heard about it. The Cubists, Futurists, Extremists, etc. Well, it's some exhibit. Some of it's good and some is rotten, if there is such a distinction. There are no rules in art, you know, so the sanest way is to say that each man may so paint as to express himself or to express a sensation or experience. . . . In other words, to show or express the way one feels things . . . Believe me, there is some movement in art. Something surely is going to happen. And to think I am here where I can see, learn, and take part in the thing my system seems to be built with. Art—such a word.[8]

Jonson's ears were attuned to the faintest whisper, his eyes to the tiniest glint of that freedom which was to be one of the major trends of twentieth-century art. It was his acute awareness that made it possible for him to pick up the meager suggestions of his future direction and develop freely according to his needs. Early phases of modern painting were about abstract ideas, whereas later developments show much of painting to be about painting. When a developmental theme appears in Jonson's Modernism, it has to do with the way he made his own transition from the former concept to the latter.

7

The Chicago Little Theatre

The problems of making a living for himself Jonson solved in many ways. Most of them he found distasteful. In his early student phase he did a variety of things to earn his way, including occasional commercial art jobs, which he had come to despise. So we can understand his joy when, at the end of March 1913, he wrote to his mother:

> I think I have a good position. And glory of it all, it is not commercial. Through Mrs. Lou Wall Moore [a member of the Jackson Park colony], I get in with the "Little Theater Co." You know what it is, don't you? A new idea, so to speak, in dramatic art. I believe it harmonizes with modern or the new art. I feel it's a rare opportunity to get in with these people for it will mean a chance to learn and at the same time paint for it will not take all my time.
>
> The job is that of all around handy man, management of scenes and lights, dressing rooms, suping, etc. I'll get $10.00 a week. . . .
>
> Goodbye commercial worry!!! Is this God's will? It must be.[1]

Maurice Browne and Ellen Van Volkenburg in founding the Chicago Little Theatre helped to initiate the little theater movement in America. Browne, later to be a director in New York and a successful producer in London, wrote of Jonson's coming to the little theater group:

> Raymond Jonson had been sent to us soon after the theatre opened by Bror Nordfeldt, the painter, when we were desperately

seeking a young Hercules who would masterfully unite in himself stage-designer, stage-manager, stage-carpenter, scene-painter, scene-shifter, electrician and, on occasion, actor. "Jonson," said Nordfeldt, "wants to become a painter; he is about twenty. He came to me as a student a few months ago, knowing nothing and thinking that he knew everything. He is immensely lovable; and I believe that he has genius."[2]

Jonson was the Chicago Little Theatre's stage designer for the rest of its brief five-year life. Of his involvement with it, he has written, "It was there that in a sense, I grew up. I have always considered it my main source of education and I believe it was there that I came to realize to some considerable extent the purpose and meaning of the idealistic and true approach to any creative art."[3]

His letters during 1913, his first year with the theater, tell us of his experiences and feelings and the excitement they engendered:

April 20. The theatre job is fine. They are so nice and good to me. Real artists, as it were. . . .

April 28. Just think how much better it is to know and feel . . . have ideals and the backbone to work them out . . . than to have riches. Books, music, arts, oh how sublime. Sensations—how great a thing to have. It's worth more than all the superficial supposed somethings in the world. . . .

May 14. The new play is set and last night was opening night. Really the sensation was great. I took part you know. My first appearance.[4] I love sensations. I want them and I want to paint them. I am in a great place.

This is a place that is more than a theatre can ever be. It's so small and cozy and I feel so much at home here. Everybody is so nice and so appreciative one feels like really working. I have the honor of having set the stage for our new play "The Shadowy Waters" by W. B. Yeats. . . . [5] Your son is the luckiest living being in this realm. . . .

May 22. I am in the height of sensations, good diet, good company, good health, and wonderful possibilities. . . . Life is great and I shall make and get the most out of it and, I hope, through the love of all that is best in art—all arts. I think that is what riches are. . . .

Nov. 1. I have become so interested and excited over the thing, not as a theatre but as an art, and when I say art I mean in relation to my art. It seems every day strengthens the common sympathy in ideas and ideals existing between Mr. Browne and me. Here he is, trying, experimenting to make the stage, not a financial, cold, superficial, imitative realism for feeding the people to gain their purse, but a decoration, a painting, a work of sculpture, a note, color, simplicity—all in one. . . .

Nov. 7. Color! —well, dear ones, you can't imagine the great opportunities one has before him in art. Color, yes we really have color at the theatre. I run the lights, of course. Here we handle real color light. We play with it. We work wonders with it. I believe we are doing what no one else, in this country at least, is doing—"stage decoration". . . . We've thrown realism to the winds. If Belasco wants realism he may search the winds.

Why copy? Why not create? And so my art is consistent—no, I do not mean that, I mean the art of the theatre and painting may, can, and are helping each other. . . .

It was an exciting time in the American theater, particularly the part of it devoted to the setting of the stage, for a new concept was making its appearance. In December 1914 Sam Hume brought an exhibition of stage models and supplementary design materials to the Art Institute of Chicago.[6] Jonson, near the beginning of his second season as a stage designer, wrote to his family:

There is a Theatre exhibit at the Art Institute. We were invited to exhibit as we are the only Art Theatre in Chicago. My stuff shows off to good advantage. I have a model stage set with one of our scenes and lighted. There are 26 others [stage models] and it is indeed an honor to be represented there. Then I have a large canvas of a "Pierrot," posters, designs of stage settings, costume designs, etc., all original—the others are practically all photographs. I have a whole wall space to myself and hung it the way I wanted.[7]

This was Jonson's first inclusion in a stagecraft exhibition. Concerning it, Maurice Browne wrote, "Hume's exhibition revolutionized American stage-design; but I question whether one per cent of its fifteen thousand visitors had ever bought seats for any play staged by any of the three American designers whose work was shown: Hume himself, Robert Edmond Jones and Raymond Jonson."[8] The American stage has not been the same since for here was introduced the new principle that stage decoration is an art and that its functioning must be as an art.

Several stagecraft exhibitions later, the New York Bourgeois Galleries in 1919 presented thirteen American designers. In the catalog for the exhibition, Jonson wrote, under the title "The New Stage Designing":

> The success of the new stage designing is to a certain extent dependent upon the play. The modern successful play is usually trash, as far as true art is concerned, so of what profit is a new motive in the background? Well, it serves as an example of something better. It helps the play along, and is more bearable to look at. Above all, it is more in relation to the action, and comes nearer to reality being farther from realism.
>
> For me the new movement means a striving for complete unity in the theatre: a new form of expression. . . ."[9]

Many years later, Jonson spoke at greater length on the subject:

> Our theater was a hotbed of discussion about correlation in the arts. A great deal along that line was achieved. The overall aim at the Little Theatre was the unified stage picture. Without the unity of the whole there is no great art. In applying that thought to the theater we saw that the synthesis of many factors became a necessity. At the Little Theatre the effort was made to achieve that synthesis. We held the hope that it wouldn't be the case of performers *and* audience but of an experience jointly and simultaneously experienced. Sometimes this rapport was attained and I believe that true art was the result.
>
> One of my deepest motivations was to leave the imagination

of the audience free, for I wanted those who saw my stagings to be participants, to enter into the setting and play, no longer mere viewers but actors themselves, so to speak, feeling and moving with the action of the play. There was always the effort to have everything on stage a unity, so I also thought of a higher unity, that between the actors and the audience. Whether this hope was ever achieved with any consistency, I don't know, but I do know that there were times when the rapport I have mentioned, in which the entire theater seemed to coalesce into this emotional unity, was unmistakable and overwhelming.[10]

In an extended article in *Theatre Arts Magazine* for July 1920 Eunice Tietjens wrote in part:

Lighting is Mr. Jonson's specialty. Primarily a painter, he brings to the theatre an essentially visual mind, and concentrates on the two purely visual factors through which the central rhythm of the play passes, decoration and lighting. But decoration, once the key is set, remains relatively a static thing . . . while lighting has the added interest of being constantly changing, constantly responsive to the central rhythm. . . . So Jonson concentrates on lighting.

Under the spur of necessity he varied his style to suit the varied repertory of the theatre, designing and executing . . . sets for Greek tragedy, modern poetic drama, realistic comedy, historical plays, interpretive dancing, genre pieces and puppet plays. . . . Yet, though he adapted himself to many styles, he remained at his best in poetic drama—whether classic or modern. . . . With real tragedy and poetic fantasy he is always at home and in his theatrical work it is on sets like that for *Medea*, *The Trojan Women* and Cloyd Head's *Grotesques*[11]—which he himself considers his most successful set—that his fame rests. . . ."[12]

The enrichment that Jonson brought to the theater, the theater brought to his life as a man and an artist. It was while he was with the theater group that he met his future wife. In letters to his mother he told a bit of the story:

Figure 5. *Auditorium of The Chicago Little Theatre.* 1915.
Watercolor, 15x21 inches. Shown beyond the proscenium is an
outline of the setting for *The Trojan Women* of Euripides.
Photograph, Thomas E. Zudick.

Figure 6. *Design for the Stage Set for* Grotesques *by Cloyd
Head.* 1915. Watercolor, 13½x18½ inches.

How am I to tell you of the most wonderful thing in the world? . . . I have dreamed of perfect love, I have wondered, I have desired it, I have doubted it. I haven't really known what it was and now . . . I see, I feel, I know, and I give and take and find the ultimate joy in both for they are one. It is the perfect balance, unity and understanding. We shall work together. . . .

Vera White you know by my other letter. No, you can't know her till you've met her and when you know her you will love her. . . . She has been secretary and about everything else at the theater. She writes. I will say she's a poet. And then, she understands, she helps, she encourages my work and me. And personality—wonderful![13]

They were married on 25 December 1916. It was a marriage given to art first and their personal necessities and conveniences second.

In the Retrospective Collection there are thirteen paintings done as anniversary gifts for Vera (see Figure 7), another for a birthday. They are intimate and personal celebrations of Jonson's love, appreciation, and reverence for her, and his gratitude for their life together in a partnership devoted to his art. The memorial works, though they were private communications, have characteristics that tie in with the work being done at the times they were painted.

Jonson's involvement with the Chicago Little Theatre was like a pressure cooker in its effect on his development as an artist. It was an association which greatly shortened the time of his technical development through its extraordinary demands on his skills and inventiveness. There was a heightening of the intensity of his feeling about art from his constant contact and interaction with people as creative and passionate in their interests and devotion as he was; people who, for the most part, were more mature and sure of themselves, qualities which Jonson, by his nature, strove to match and even surpass. Consequently, it is not surprising that there was a quick upward surge in the development of his craft and his maturing as an artist.

He seemed to be in a continual state of excitement as witnessed by the exclamatory nature of his letters to his parents:

I am well and happy—paint, work—no, play—sleep and eat; think, ah yes—imagination runs quite wild nowadays. . . . I find so

Figure 7.   *Twenty (Anniversary for Vera)*. 1936. Oil, 19x13 inches.

much to paint. Everyone at the theatre is willing to pose—and such costumes and color!——oh, I rave.[14]

Virtually from the outset this phase of Jonson's work is particularly marked by a series of strong works which use the human figure as a dominant motif (see Plate 1 and Figures 8–10). Whatever these portraits—or, as he preferred to call them, characterizations—meant to the artist because of personal relationships with the sitters, they had a larger meaning in that they demanded of him certainty of execution. The paintings demonstrate a flair for composition. They are inventive, dramatic, and give every indication that the use of color as a projector of mood and character was becoming a part of his permanent painting vocabulary.

In the portrait characterizations we note the results of the rapid growth of his resources. The figure is often posed against a flamboyant background of large formalized flowers or other wallpaper motifs. Or it may be set in a richly developed atmosphere accomplished by a multitude of small dabs and spots of color more evocative of light and mood than flatly applied single colors would be.

Whatever the treatment of pattern and color, they are merged into the brushing and the overall look of the surface. The integration of motifs, color, and treatment of the paint itself, particularly the last, into a major source of effect became obsessive with Jonson in his pursuit of *quality*° as an indispensable ingredient of the work of art.

The colorful and dramatic treatment of the characterizations speak of the theatric ambience in which Jonson had been living. The equal attention given to the sitter's environment as well as to the sitter and the formal treatment of both make the paintings something more than insights into human character.

The characterizations were part of the harvest of his time spent with the little theater group. The last of them was done in 1919. His interest in the person as subject dwindled off into a few portraits in charcoal. The human figure was to appear at intervals in his paintings, but it was used compositionally in varying degrees of abstraction.

°Here and throughout the text words such as *quality* and *design* are italicized to indicate that they include or exclude meanings they have in common usage. Individualized by Jonson they must be given special weight.

Figure 8. *The Lady (Mary Williams)*. 1918. Oil, 48x38 inches.

Figure 9.   *Miriam Kiper—A Characterization.* 1919. Oil, 42x38 inches.

Figure 10.   *The Sailor (Erik Smith)*. 1919. Oil, 60x42 inches.

Meanwhile, another phase of his painting had been in process. The summer of 1917 had included a soul-stirring visit to the Colorado Rockies. The physical thrust of mountain structures, the vastness of space, the clarity and brilliance of western light provided an indelible impact on the consciousness and imagination of the painter. One of the results was *Light* (Figure 11).

Exhibited throughout the Midwest in the early twenties, *Light* received favorable notices. Maurice Block in the *Omaha Evening World Herald* wrote:

> What a bold attempt to portray light in the canvas of that name. Technically there is no more difficult problem. He accomplishes his end by contrasting light with other forces, namely the weight and solidity of rock.[15]

Another writer, in the *Minneapolis Journal,* commented that:

> A Jonson rock has its roots in the dawn of time. His sky is the glorious thing the first beholding eye of man grew accustomed to. His sun is a thing of infinite radiance.[16]

Light was purchased in 1925 by John Curtis Underwood[17] and presented to the Museum of New Mexico at Santa Fe. Anywhere else in the world this colorful work might seem to be a staged thing, but in its New Mexican home it epitomizes the clarity, the grandeur of the primeval forces of sun and land that are dominant in the Southwest.

This painting, although an exciting work in its own right, is also an appropriate introduction to a subject that has held Jonson's interest throughout his painting career. *Light,* if not the first, was an early manifestation of the painting of light as subject, or part of the subject, and the exploration of its possibilities as a component of Jonson's esthetic unity through a variety of technical and conceptual approaches. The way light is used in this canvas may scarcely be called "natural light" but nevertheless it is projected from the sun. Light spreads out in expanding circles crossed by the bands of a brilliant sunburst. It is all representational, though far from realistic. In this representation sunrises, sunsets, and high noons, reactions, whether physical or esthetic, that light can arouse, imaginings, are assembled and combined into a single expression: a metaphor of light.

Figure 11. *Light.* 1917. Oil, 45x42 inches. Museum of New Mexico, Museum of Fine Arts, Santa Fe. Photograph, Ken Cobean.

This kind of treatment of light in Jonson's work was an expanding thing, so that this early painting is like the point of departure for an extensive, prolonged study of how paint can be made to express light and light's influence. It is little wonder that a person who looks for the familiar or reassuring thing in paintings should nevertheless find in such works something beyond the surface aspect and experience feelings that transcend the mundane to enter a realm that can be termed the spiritual.

For this is what Jonson intended when he used the word *spiritual* in reference to painting, namely that the individual, the viewer, may be lifted beyond the simple materialism of life. When this happens there is a meeting of the artist and the viewer of his art, for the emotion felt by the latter is akin to that of the former. "In every genuine work of art," he said, "the ecstasy of the creator is the origin and that of the receiver is the fulfillment."[18] Such a condition of rapport is possible particularly in the case of absolute painting when the viewer is willing to shed his inhibitions and prejudices and simply "feel" the work of art. This kind of feeling Jonson considered to be a spiritual rather than a materialistic experience and the painting that could evoke it to arise from the spiritual rather than the physical or material.

What Jonson eventually came to was not light as subject but light as a mysterious substance which seems to emanate from the painting itself. In Jonson's words, "If successful the overall effect of the work would be of unearthiness, of light not from our sun but from unknown sources. Therefore, rather than the physical, the spiritual would carry the load."[19]

8

The MacDowell Colony

After the Chicago Little Theatre closed, Jonson felt the pinch between earning a living and finding time to paint. The Jonsons were living mostly on hope in April of 1919 when this entry appears in his diary:

> Our trust was built, is built, on solid ground. From some tiny hole in the sky has dropped a trip, studio, food, etc., for the summer—no, we pay our fare, that is all. Mrs. Edward MacDowell has given us a scholarship in the colony of that name. . . . A month ago we had no plans, now we have. What a glorious, happy life we lead. On the 15th of May we leave for Peterborough, New Hampshire. In the fall we expect to drop into New York. No west this time; I am sorry, too. Well, having never been in New England it ought to be a good thing.[1]

His diary entries at the colony began:

> June 1, 1919. Here we are at last. . . . We have a most delightful studio in the woods. It is called the "Adams Studio." Large north light, fireplace and plenty of room. We are all settled and ready for work. May the spirit move us deeply. The country looks good, entirely different from anything I have done. . . . In all it is most marvelous and we are happy. . . . This is a wonderful place to work.
>
> July 6, 1919. I really have accomplished very little. A great deal of rest and good food. . . . The country here is very nice—rather more dreamy and poetic than strong, rugged and

fascinating like the western mountains. It is such that my mind rather dreams along composing imaginative arrangements. I have several ideas on which I am working. It is a great joy to be free from noise and the struggle in the city. Of course I prefer the wilder large nature but grant that this is good for one's soul also. Therefore I shall work by mood and spirit—what I get—no one knows.

The First Morning (Figure 12) was completed five months after a second summer at the MacDowell Colony. His diary entry says, "It is finished and is

Figure 12. *The First Morning.* Drawing, 4¾x6½ inches in Jonson's diary. Photograph, Thomas E. Zudick. The painting is a 1920 oil, 38x48 inches. Collection Donald B. Anderson.

a great success! I am happy."[2] Happy because he was able to convey a particular mood he had experienced from the local landscape through painterly terms. The sinuous horizontals, the haze of color, the elimination and minimization of local detail that might be connected directly with a literal transcription of a particular scene are steps toward abstraction. The painting is not a scene directly from nature but emotional impressions resynthesized in terms of painting and given the look and appeal of the mood quality inherent in this type of landscape.

More important than the paintings that came from the two New England trips were other benefits. The atmosphere of the MacDowell Colony and the protected way of life led him down introspective paths where he ruminated, mulled, and tried to consolidate within himself a better picture of his future course while at the same time conceiving methods of facilitating this progress.

The period of introspection was not confined to the two stays in New Hampshire but continued on between them and after them until well into 1921. It was a period during which he took a hard critical look at his own attitude and what he was doing and as a result bore down mightily on himself as a painter.

On 7 July 1920 he wrote of a painting he was working on in Peterborough:

> I am going to build this picture. . . . I shall continue working
> on it until this entire list can be applied to it:
>> atmospheric
>> luminous
>> color
>> quality
>> richness
>> depth
>> juicyness
>> rhythm
>> spontaneity
>> interesting surface . . .
>
> To be worked on until all has been accomplished by painting over
> and over regardless of drying worries. If necessary scraping

—sandpaper and pumice stone to be used, and if necessary it will be an inch thick. . . .

The painting slowly came into existence, and by December he was able to note, "I have signed it."[3] Meanwhile, he was working on another painting and again struggling against the reluctance of his materials to accede to his demands. He decided that this second painting, like the first a seascape, was a failure and yet, the day after recording the failure, he was back at work on it.

The diary entry for 18 December 1920 says, "I have been at this thing for six months. . . . This, by the way, is the second piece of canvas. I wore out the first one. . . . Now we shall see." Two months later he was able to write, "It is finished and I am very happy with it. I know this to be one of the best things I have done."[4]

The two paintings to which the foregoing diary entries refer, *The Sea* and *Age*,[5] came from a side trip to Ogunquit, Maine, just before the second stay at the MacDowell Colony, where Jonson found material more suited to his needs. The rocky forms rising from the sea afforded a parallel to his mountain experience. They provided the kind of structural forms necessary to the synthesis of his own concept of form. *Earth Rhythms No. 3* of 1923 (Figure 15) was one of the products of his research into nature for shapes and rhythms that helped more harmoniously to formulate and build the type of unity he was after.

Paintings with such metaphorical titles as *Light* and *The First Morning* are works which in their directness and abstract character are related to the main direction of Jonson's evolution. But another group of paintings have foundations of a different sort. They represent an imaginary panorama of nature and life. Based on natural forms, they present emotional dramatizations of natural phenomena which in the paintings are communicated through a symbolical use of shapes and colors which establish moods suggested by meanings implied in the titles of the works. Some of them seem to unburden themselves of the tragic manifestations of man's relation to nature. Others depict dark moods that can become disagreeable, even frightening, with their juxtapositions of strange land forms, human forms, and creature forms picturing the forces that have their way in man's experience of the world. However, these paintings are not invariably tragic or dark of mood, for some of them are brighter and almost awesome in the

Figure 13. *Winter (Seasons Series)*. 1922. Oil, 35x45 inches.

observation of what is happening in nature. It is difficult to determine exactly where these works fit into Jonson's hopes for the direction his painting was to take. Evidently, if nothing else, they were essential as a catharsis, a type of purging of emotions burdening his views of human affairs and human fate.

One of the finest of this general group of works is *Winter (Seasons Series)* (Figure 13), a mature and beautiful painting.

On 14 March 1922 Jonson wrote in his diary:

> This afternoon I have finished and signed "Winter." I believe this is the best thing I have ever done. It is immense in every way.

It pleases me and I am satisfied. It has feeling and even thrills me. . . . I have expressed a thing I know rings true. I believe in this work absolutely. In this I have felt form. The composition is an inspiration. . . .

I don't believe I can express what the symbols are adequately for they are rather felt than thought. Looking back and sitting with it in front of me I say this—

Winter—the space of rest—old age of life. It is the time before spring when seeds sprout. The figures may be the symbol of all [human] life—the sitting female at rest, holding within the warmth of life, waiting for the male to join her. The male, horizontal, at complete rest. Principle lines horizontal—cold—no, it can't be done, that is not it, it is more, it is something else, it is greater. Why describe it?

Important as *Winter* was, it held another importance of an entirely different nature. Hung in the Annual Chicago Artists exhibition of 1923 at the Art Institute where it was awarded the Englewood Women's Club Prize, the painting was seen by Charles Morris, then at the beginning of his career at the University of Chicago. The use of symbols, which was then and continued to be a preoccupation of the philosopher, roused in Morris an appreciation and understanding which caused him to seek out the creator of this painting. The result was a lifelong friendship, a perennial and unceasing support by the younger man, who became a propagandist for the artist, and a reciprocal admiration and devotion on the part of the painter. The initial confrontation and the subsequent relationship was for Jonson a sustaining power throughout the years, in times of uncertainty and depression and in times of realization and rejoicing.

9

Declaration of Purpose

Jonson received from Chicago stimulation, knowledge, and the enrichment of his personal life, but he found other aspects of the city both irritating and frustrating. In some of his earliest letters from Chicago he noted that the city was a "pretty dirty place," that he had "a dread of dirt," and that "dirt is a pest to humanity." During the entire fourteen years of his stay in the city he constantly expressed his resentment of metropolitan uncleanliness, both the inanimate seeping, clinging, infiltrating types—smoke, dust, and soot—and the animate pushing, grasping, selfish struggling of people who were a part of the industrial, mercantile Chicago.

"One feels restless here," he wrote. "There is no calm. All is fighting and therefore one like myself, calm and peaceful, is rather swamped amid the debris."[1] He did not like the competitive and predatory activities that he saw about him. "I believe the greater part of this world is a sort of fake—that is, the inhabitants. Business, business!! Talk . . . cleverness . . . beat the other fellow to it."[2]

Jonson's irritation with the world of men was further emphasized when America was on the verge of World War I. He felt his attempt to live a constructive life was being frustrated. In reaction he registered as a conscientious objector in the draft. On 20 April 1917 he wrote to his brother Arthur:

> If we were advocates of such methods of manslaughter we
> would have good reason to be very much worried and troubled
> but, thanks be, we feel otherwise. Mother said in her letter that

they had been trying to get you to enlist, which is perfectly natural, which is also perfectly criminal. . . .

I am glad you are so definitely opposed to war. You may be assured I am also. . . . I, for one, refuse to have any connection with the doings, either directly or indirectly. . . .

I hope you also will stick to what you know and feel is right. We cannot fight for our principle because we don't believe in fighting. . . . The faithful one has only one duty and that is to be faithful.

The war ended, but Jonson was not deceived. In a long letter to Arthur on 3 August 1923 among his observations was:

We think the Mechanical Age tends to demoralize the arts. I say it emphasizes the significance of the true expression. . . . those who bear the torch of light create the record of the purest thought of a period. We live in an atmosphere of butchery and running blood whose smells enter our very homes and as a protest some of us are developed toward a greater purity as a natural result of opposition. Contrast, that is the basis of all visibility.

Hardly more than a decade after armistice ended the war, Jonson became aware that the world had again gone askew. The Jonsons had always been poor. The frugality demanded, the limitations and restrictions caused by the economic decay in the depression of the thirties burdened them less than the threat against the grand design. His letters reveal his attitude:

If there were more of the sort of idealism I believe in and live and have talked so much about there would be no more wars nor any "depressions" either. If the beauty I stand for was common property of everyone, the social system at least would be a little cleaner and offer at least a reason for its existence. I see well the situation. If one has a beauty that the world needs then he should see that the world gets it. I sometimes feel I would like to jump into the mess. But think of the time and energy it would take. I am for putting that into the work itself. Yes, it is quite a problem; how at the same time [to] create and live that beauty. That is the question.[3]

We seem to be at the mercy of all that is wrong. All that I ask is that I be allowed to do my work. I have reached a place where any time being or doing things that are not a living part of one's self and work is a crime.[4]

Within me things are boiling. I see so much injustice and lack of attention to things that seem to me to matter, and I personally have such a struggle to accomplish a few of the things that seem worthy of accomplishment, that at times the whole business of trying to live beautifully in a man-made ugliness seems hopeless. One aspect of the reason for painting seems to be that a kind of oasis is necessary through this kind of effort because of the lack in general of the finer things possible in life. So I suppose we at times make a protest through creating something that is beautiful and moving. But when opposition and hatred attack from all sides, it becomes difficult to keep dignified through completely ignoring it. Frustration is a devastating ogre. So some of the work I am doing is a kind of challenge to existing conditions. . . .

Even so I feel we are living in an age as never before existed. It is a struggle between the great and the cheap. Which will win out? We know not and can only hope that the great will and in that hope we struggle on through opposition of every kind.[5]

By the end of the thirties the United States was pulling itself out of the depression, but in Europe the stage was being set for one of the greatest tragedies in Jonson's era, the developments that led up to and through the Second World War. Jonson's reaction was immediate and vigorous.

I end my year with the hope that the fools in Europe and Asia will before another year is out have hung themselves so that the rest of civilization can live in peace. I dedicate my time—my effort—my thoughts and my feelings to the highest ideal of love—brotherhood and peace on this our only earth. May it contribute to the total desire to abstain from hate and fear and may we find ourselves in a world a year from now that is working for constructive ends and not this deplorable condition of complete destruction that now exists.

For 25 years I have struggled to exist in a world that is against a pure concept of love and peace. During these years my effort has been constructive and I have hoped that it would contribute to the heightening of civilization and the freeing of humanity. But humanity has failed me. But I shall continue—continue on to the end. . . . Love and religion have failed as expressed by power and so we can well dedicate our effort toward an abstract vision of the ideal that underlies the truth in them. I see now that the only effort that survives is the constructive one. My power in the past has been the opposite of what is now commonly considered power. But I hope that this different power—this power that raises instead of lowers life will be able to function full blast. I hope the visions will come to me so that I may be the humble servant of that beautiful strength and courage in order to record the highest in man and that some portion of it may be saved for the new civilization that will have to start all over. The present seems hopeless but it is not and the future may blossom and the whole panorama of living survive, decently and honestly. And so may this vehicle—me—be able to stick by the job of recording our real makeup, life in the full.[6]

Thus Jonson affirmed his faith in life and art. It is significant that when he so wrote, he was on the threshold of the most important period of his life and art. The affirmation was not merely so many words but a declaration of purpose. He proceeded forthwith to a demonstration of its viability in the works he created.

10

"Design"

From the outset of his life in art Jonson was receptive to those trends of modern art that reached him. As his student days progressed and his attitude as an artist developed, he began to form an approach that considered the current aspects of modern art. In Chicago his access to good examples of recent and current trends of national and international contemporary art was limited. Nevertheless, his contact was sufficient. The fertilization was there, and eventually the plant blossomed as he developed through a number of phases to the clear projection of his intent.

Even though the realization of the full nature and possibilities of modern art was not extensive in his work during the years before Santa Fe, the implications of it were constantly in his thoughts and intentions. What he did and learned in the early years led to his ultimate breakthrough into an abstract idiom in painting and an attempt to express in words that which he had come to feel as the primary forces in the art of painting. He needed to find for himself a term that would sum up the use of those forces and express what he had discovered, experienced, and learned. He did not coin a new word but to an existing word gave extended meaning and emphasis. He chose to use the word *design* to indicate a *unifying principle* which through its application became the main direction of his personal and his artistic life.

To Jonson life meant harmony. His ideal indicated to him that the social structure should and could establish a harmony in rapport with that of the individual. This harmony he believed to be an essential order which, as an artist, he should attempt to express by clarifying it and making it visible.

As the visible essential in his art, Jonson evolved a *unifying principle,* conceiving of it as a formal property which has its own significance as a concept. No casual definition can illuminate this theory of *design* as Jonson felt it, thought of it, believed in it, worked at it, and tried to live it.

The artist starts with feeling. To be an artist he must know how to trust his intuitions and how to follow his instincts. It is not sufficient merely to insert himself into the course of the centuries-long flow of the art expression. He must impose on it what he has learned, what he has seen and felt, and bring to it what he individually is and his sense of the destiny of man—both the individual man and the race of man. Everything in his experience must be bent to the artist's primary justification for being an artist, namely the expression of the thing felt and the extension of the meanings of art.

The word "design" has had many prior applications in art. None of them reach to its meaning as we shall use it in reference to Jonson's thinking and processes in painting or its demonstration in the finished works. The paintings are themselves its best definition. The sensitive observer is moved by it even though he has not been alerted to look for it, since it is a thing that in every successful application pervades the painting. In moments of enthusiasm and inspiration, Jonson has used *design* as a synonym for what he called, at one time or another, "my idea." The intention is that it should encompass and express all the feelings he sought to compress into the spaces and colors potential to canvas and paint, that it should stand as a symbol in the world of human affairs, and that it should sum up the means, methods, and objectives involved in the art of painting.

It is not possible to isolate each of the significances which he has attached to the word, for it is an inclusive term which embraces the art instinct, the art urge, and the art expression. Whether in reference to the states of humanity and its environment or to the particulars of what was at the moment a painter's problem, it does mean a way of living, seeing, and feeling. This *unifying principle* applies not only to a way of painting but also to a way of living. Consequently, there was involved an attitude which suggested that although the goal might not be reached, the trip should be a satisfying one.

Jonson felt that he could use *design* to imply a different type of organization than that indicated in the aspects of design previously known to art. There would be a difference in procedure since the means used would not be the use of a familiar cultural convention or context but a distinctive way of working unique to each painting, and there would be a direct emotional appeal to the viewer's sensibility.

The attempt would be to produce an image at once personal and universal. Jonson felt that the artist could extend *design* into painting without reliance on motifs extracted from a known context and consequently could extend painting into *design*. He wanted to set up a painting in such a way that it could function as a unit; that content and the elements of painting should be so integrated that the result would be a direct source of experience. The influences leading to *design* were manifold.

11

Influences

The inner promptings of order and unity were with him from the beginning when, as an art student, he first attempted to solve the problems of painting. The call for order, the desire for clarity in art and life were deep-seated in Jonson's character. The clear light and vast spaces of the Midwest of his childhood, and of the West where he traveled and has spent the major part of his life, had a lasting influence on the effects of space and light that were eventually produced in his paintings.

The western environment, ample, limitless, encouraged an inward look in the artist. He was prompted to replace minutiae with large conceptual ideas. There was a great sense of wonder, of starkness, a desire to break narrow boundaries, to widen the scope of vision, and to generalize in a world given to detail and fact.

In his contact with B. J. O. Nordfeldt, fortunately early in his career, Jonson learned the importance of spontaneity, a contrast to the rigidities of art school classrooms. He was stimulated to desire simplicity, directness, strong composition, and essential form.[1] The enthusiasm for painting which Nordfeldt exuded and his disdain for the realism of the majority of painters about him made an impact on the younger man which probably influenced him to treasure an individual and independent approach in his own work. Out of all this he developed emotional identification with the act of painting.

The influence of the Chicago Little Theatre on Jonson's development cannot be overestimated. There, in the reaction against the period's popular "realistic" theater, cluttered, itemized, naturalistic, he participated in and contributed to the concept of the theater as a synthesis of arts. At the most impressionable time of his life he learned how to integrate diverse factors of production. His settings, costumes, and lighting became as much a part of the play as the author's words and the actors' performances.

The effort to attain in the theater a unity of all the elements entering into the production of a play was reflected in his thinking about the art of painting and made a contribution to the ideas which, in the future, coalesced in his theory of *design.* In the theater he learned to incorporate the factors of artistic multiplicity into a unified, single, direct impression and the value of an immediate dramatic effect. The mood, color, movement, and excitement of stage production pulled him away from local environment mindedness and turned him to fantasy, metaphor, and, ultimately, abstraction.

In March 1913 the Armory Show, moving from New York, opened in Chicago. It exhibited a wide variety of American contemporaries together with equally wide developments in modern art from Europe. Already chafing at the academic nature of the experience at the Chicago Academy, Jonson found in the Armory Show a release from the residue of the school's influence, thus buttressing what he had gained from Nordfeldt and the theater. He didn't turn to imitation of the works that had moved him nor did he fly off on a tangent. Instead, he began the slow course of his individual development even though, at the time, the goal toward which he would strive was but dimly seen.

Of considerable importance to his thinking was the book *Art* by Clive Bell. In it, for the first time, Jonson found formulated in words some of the ideas that had been churning in his mind, ideas he himself could not, as yet, verbalize. Among things that Bell wrote which Jonson appropriated to his own context were sayings such as "Art is the creation of significant form, and simplification is the liberating of what is significant from what is not," and "In a work of art nothing is relevant but what contributes to formal significance." "Every form in a work of art," Bell wrote, "has, then, to be made aesthetically significant; also every form has to be made a part of a significant whole. . . . This organization of forms into a significant whole is called Design.[2]

It is not beyond likelihood that many years in the future, having developed his theories about a *unifying principle,* Jonson too should choose to use the term "design," influenced thereto by the author of *Art;* although *design,* as Jonson used it, was perhaps more individualized.

While at the MacDowell Colony in 1919, because the landscape at Peterborough failed to stimulate him, he worked slowly and gave much time to the contemplation of things far removed from that scene. He sought to clarify for himself the thing that was stirring in his mind even as it seemed to elude him. In his diary he asked:

> Why should not a picture be that rhythmic conscious conception of nature that accident rarely accomplishes? Every object has its high moment. Every combination of objects [has its] highest moment. That is, things as they usually are, are not as significant as those things can be when properly manifested through a rhythmic unified whole. . . . There is a fine relation between the inner and outer. To grasp these all-important characteristics and weave them into a rhythmic whole which moves and calls forth the spirit of each object used is the proper conception of composition.[3]

When in 1920 he returned for a second summer at the MacDowell Colony, following a brief but fruitful stay at Ogunquit, Maine, Jonson's analytical trend continued:

> I've been thinking that the creation of an entirely abstract [nonrepresentational] composition would be an excellent thing. Why shouldn't planes of color in gradation, properly arranged, make beauty? I doubt whether the forms of nature if rightly interpreted can be improved upon. Nevertheless, it seems to me that the attempt to create abstract ones would be a very good study.[4]

In the spring of 1921, moved by an exhibition at the Art Institute of works by Nicholas Roerich, Jonson was able to get a clearer view and more cogent expression of the ideas he was trying to formulate.

> I find that the work that is simply for itself and not a design for something else is by far the most complete and satisfying. Here we have the ultimate use of art. The work for itself—to stand as the

expression of an emotion, the abstract spiritual ego of the individual. . . . What I mean is that indispensible something which deals with the spirit. This art should be recognized as fundamental, should be thought of outside all physical aspects. It is the great love. It can have no use outside of feeding the spirit.[5]

It was in August of the same year that he received a copy of Kandinsky's *The Art of Spiritual Harmony*.[6] Here was a confirmation from an artist who had pondered deeply on the very subject to which his own thoughts had been turning.

I have spent the last two entire days reading and digesting Kandinsky's "The Art of Spiritual Harmony." It is the greatest book concerning art I have ever read. It is immense. One cannot, if he be wise, but accept and believe in the truth he puts forth. It is a task to take in the significance of it all. I believe we must sooner or later know him to be right, at least in theory—and that is the point, theory. And then what about practice? To be able to live and actually work in the spiritual is, of course, a great ideal and one to hope and work for.[7]

What possibly can be the meaning of this word "spiritual" with reference to an expression that seems by its nature to be predominantly material? The work of art itself is an object seen in the objective universe. But the artist comes to the realization that perhaps beyond the material aspect there are special heightening possibilities; that a painting, being a thing in itself, can arouse in the beholder thoughts and ideas which originate as a result of the painting. What Kandinsky did was to find a different sort of spiritual value than the obvious one of "sacred art" and make it central to the art of painting. Kandinsky's drift toward theosophy was never shared by Jonson, but Jonson's sense of the mystical permitted him to be stimulated by Kandinsky into a recognition of the goal he sought and the means for reaching it. That he eventually arrived at a different way of stating a similar aspiration emphasizes anew the scope and variety of art.

12

New Mexico

During the years Jonson lived in Chicago he got away from the city as often as possible. His choice of direction was west. His most ecstatic responses to nature came from experiences with the structural grandeur of the western mountains.

In 1922 he was able to spend the entire summer at Santa Fe, New Mexico. It was John Curtis Underwood's idea and insistence, backed up by the purchase of paintings to help defray the expenses, which led to this, as it turned out, momentous summer. In this new environment his spirit soared, and it was here that he had the third of those "visions" that he thought of as spiritual experiences, as recounted in his Chili Club talk:

> Santa Fe, 1922. While visiting Santa Fe for the first time another such experience, but advanced in character, was granted me. During a two or three day camping and sketching trip to Buckman, I suddenly realized that this was a turning point and a new beginning was necessary and that the results of this would be along the lines sensed but not really known back in 1911. This necessitated a long course of study and work in connection with our environment here. Through this I sensed a means of arriving at plastic design. Therefore, it was necessary to move permanently into this country which was finally accomplished in 1924. For the next several years much work was done directly from the landscape which now in retrospect appears to be a part of the general foundation for what was to follow. Much of the work from 1922 to 1929 was semi-abstract.[1]

When he returned to Chicago, he carried with him "about fifty fairly decent things," of which some thirty-eight oil sketches and watercolors have survived, from the Santa Fe area. He also carried with him the determination to consummate the plans for a home and studio in New Mexico. While there he had been visited by his mother, en route to her home in Portland from a trip to New York. Entering into his enthusiasm, she had lent him the money to buy a building site in Santa Fe. In Chicago, for the first and last time in his life, he set out on a deliberate course of selling as much of his work as possible in order to raise funds for the forthcoming venture, even though it involved actions which were abhorrent to him. Eventually he purged himself of the stigma of selling which this period of approximately a year inflicted on him.

At the same time he was looking at and thinking about the Santa Fe landscape studies. At this point he began using a governing system or framework of space division different in concept from what he had previously called "composition" and set to work exploiting this manifestation of a *unifying principle* which participated in formulating his *design* idea.

> I have recently come in touch with an idea of a geometrical framework or governing system of direction in composition. . . . I shall have to apply it in my own way as that is what I believe in. . . .
>
> I have always felt that there should be a governing sense of arrangement, that is, that a composition usually should have order and most often a simple basic motive of spaces, and interesting variety of shapes and spaces, a balance of line direction. . . .
>
> So often in a composition one is conscious of so confused arrangement of direction that there is no order. I feel one must have order. Therefore, why shouldn't one plan the limits of directions, space and space edges adhering to such a plan? . . .
>
> The dividing up of the area must be mathematically correct so that all portions of one's area will be in relation and balance. This gives the first step—a guiding framework. Then comes the relationship to it of the interior of forms themselves—the composition within form. Then there is the balancing and construction of light and

shade or light and dark in relation to this resulting in a consistent massing together of all the elements of one's entire single work—providing one is an artist, that being the first necessity in the proper use of such a principle.

Of course, one's idea and material used determine the particular diagram. . . . To be sure, it is nothing new. Geometry has always been connected in some way or other with art. But I see in this something concrete. I wouldn't accept it unless I felt that here is a great principle. . . .[2]

At approximately the same time that Jonson "came in touch" with this idea of a governing system, Jay Hambidge was writing about and teaching his system called Dynamic Symmetry. It was based on a careful study of the art and architecture of the Periclean period in Greece. Hambidge showed that the Greeks had employed a mathematical system of proportion based not only on the logic which was the essence of the Greek mind, but also on what they believed to be the condition of nature itself. Jonson recognizes that he might well have used Dynamic Symmetry to advantage, had he known of it at the time, in the early years of working out his *design* theory. As it was, the scheme he did use was a simple one that invited great freedom in its application.

One of the results of his interest in the space-planning scheme was the beginning of the *Earth Rhythms* series (see Figures 14 and 15). The *Earth Rhythms,* with the exception of Number 3 which went back to his Ogunquit sea sketches, were based on the material he sketched in New Mexico. From this point on his paintings show the effects of the new point of departure. The shapes delineated are still natural forms, often specific items of landscape, but they have lost their local identities by being meshed into a planned space which relates the subject matter more to the painting space than to the natural space from which it came. Now, working on this basis with the consciousness of a defined principle of organization, the ideas which were to develop further the concept of *design* became clearer.

Three of the four works Jonson painted in 1923 made use of the theory as described in his diary, but he did not employ a strict application of his space division system beyond 1925. However, it served a useful purpose in the development of the idea of a *unifying principle* and the clarification of

Figure 14. *Earth Rhythms No. 3.* Pencil drawing, 4¾x6¼ inches
in Jonson's diary showing the "scaffolding" designed for the
painting.

Figure 15. *Earth Rhythms No. 3.* 1923. Oil, 32x40 inches.

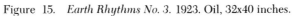

his ideas concerning organization and composition, for it very quickly became embedded in his consciousness, and soon it was engulfed in the wider, more absorbing range of possibilities of the *design* theory.

Early in 1925 Jonson was at last installed in his Santa Fe studio. The few works painted in the early part of 1923 and the entirely unproductive year of 1924 when he was building his residence and studio were behind him. Now he could set to work. Considering what had gone before, the first new work was an unexpected production. *Composition Four—Melancholia* (Figure 16) is an advance into abstraction of a different character than that of any previous painting. There are elements in it derived, one supposes, from the same sources as earlier works, but everything is used in a different way. The shapes may originate in part from nature, but the expression here is of something beyond natural shapes, for it reflects the pressure of an inner turmoil, the "agony" of having been away from painting for more than a year. It is an expression that calls from the depths of consciousness demanding purgation of his frustrations and redemption from the "sin" of having been for so long a constructor of a building instead of paintings.

Jonson sketched from nature using pencils, charcoal, lithographic crayon, watercolors, and oils. Hundreds of such studies explored the shapes, rhythms, and relationships of the landscape. From his first encounter with the environment around Santa Fe, yearly for fifteen years he tried to capture on paper an enduring moment in the life of the terrain. From this grew a compendium of forms, reference works to which he could turn as the need arose. He added the word "Sketch" to the titles of most of the paintings so done from nature, for he did not consider them to be finished works. Rather, aside from their function as sources of forms and ideas for paintings, they acquainted him with the environment in which he moved, gave him the feeling of the land, the quality of the atmosphere, and served to keep his hand in at working with natural shapes. Many of these "sketches" could have stood, as such works frequently have for painters, as finished paintings. Some of them are fairly literal transcriptions of the things seen at a specific place and time. Instinctively, however, the artist imposed on them an order that nature seldom accomplishes. In the works in which he made use of these landscape sketches there are apt to be borrowings from a number of them, often enough from different places, for he used whatever appealed to him, whatever its source. In most cases he did not want the finished painting

Figure 16. *Composition Four—Melancholia.* 1925. Oil, 46x38 inches. Collection Irvin L. Bernstein, Philadelphia, Pa. Photographer unknown.

to relate to any specific locality but to express a synthesis or generalization in the delineation of the emotions the materials stimulated.

Near Alcalde of 1936 (Figure 17) and *Near Tesuque* of 1937 (Figure 18) may be taken as typical of Jonson's drawings from nature. There are fifteen of these on-the-spot drawings in the Retrospective Collection out of the hundreds he made. By doing these many drawings, he assimilated, he absorbed, and he came to recognize his own material. At the same time he learned to impose on this scene his feelings, deep responses, and interpretations of the things depicted. This became more evident when the materials of the drawings were transposed and recreated into the contents of the paintings. More and more the shapes lost their local identities as they were transformed to the needs of the painting, but throughout the twenties and into the thirties nature as such was rarely absent from his painting.

The first beneficiary of all the sketching and study of the shapes and rhythms of Jonson's favorite locale was the series called *Earth Rhythms* and subsequently those other groups which grew out of or succeeded them. *Earth Rhythms No. 6* (Figure 19) is representative of the series. Concerning it, Jonson wrote:

> *Earth Rhythms No. 6* (1925) is based on formations near Chimayo, New Mexico. In this painting we have a slight degree of abstraction. The forms are easily recognized as earth erosion, sky, etc. But all the means used are adapted to a certain concept of color, movement, space, light and dark and with at least some semblance of order resulting from the way in which it is planned.[3]

Much the same sort of thing could be said of all the *Earth Rhythms* paintings. Similarly, what he wrote in his diary concerning the first two of them is to a large extent applicable to the entire series, for although the emphasis on various elements might shift so far as the individual works were concerned, both the general attitude and objective were consistent throughout. It was in the resolution of the "confused rhythm of forms" of which he wrote that this series of works made their contribution to the development of Jonson's art.

> There is a confused rhythm of forms running through my head. And most amazing, they tend toward abstraction—the spirit of the thing in its most salient elements. Is not rhythm of the whole just

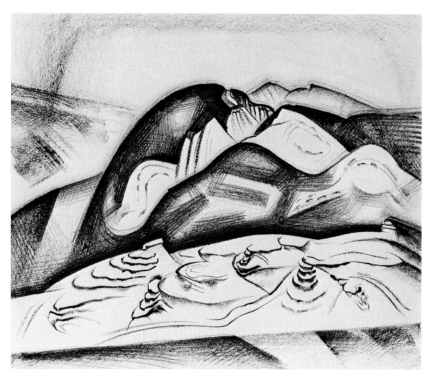

Figure 17. *Near Alcalde.* 1936.
Lithographic crayon drawing, 19x23 inches.

Figure 18. *Near Tesuque.* 1937.
Lithographic crayon drawing, 19x23 inches.

Figure 19. *Earth Rhythms No. 6.* 1925. Oil, 37x40 inches.

Figure 20. *Cloud Forms and Mesas No. 3.* 1928. Oil, 33x44 inches.

about the first to consider? And I feel one must not be too conscious about one's means or manner. It is the subconscious mind speaking through the conscious that we want.

So if by any chance I have managed to keep this thing pure, the rhythms as such should ring true. They may mean nothing by themselves. They should mean everything as a whole.[4]

Concurrently, there were other groups such as three *Cloud Forms and Mesas* (Figure 20), four *Cliff Dwellings* (Figure 21), and three *Pueblo Series* (Figure 22), paintings all done during the three years 1926–28.

These many works which dominate the mid and late twenties evidence the rich legacy bestowed by the nature sketches. The last two groups additionally incorporate the architecture of a group of mankind able to live harmoniously with that nature. So insistent was the exaltation of the landscape that in looking at the reproductions of these paintings one might

Figure 21. *Cliff Dwellings No. 3.* 1927.
Oil, 48x38 inches. Photographer unknown.

Figure 22. *Pueblo Series—Taos.* 1926. Oil, 38x48 inches.

wonder if the possibilities could ever be exhausted. Not that Jonson's aim was to exhaust the material. What he was after were the answers to questions he had asked himself in his diary, such as, "Why should not a picture be that rhythmic conscious conception of nature that accident rarely accomplishes?"[5]

Beginning in the mid twenties the southwestern landscape aroused him, inspired him, and sent him off on the exciting search for expression of the sensations it stimulated. At the outset he had written in his diary:

> In expressing my idea of this country I struggled especially to obtain a unity—a unity of all the means used [such] as form, design, color, rhythm, and line.[6]

And five years later he reported that the "struggle" continued:

It is a struggle to organize a unit that bangs with the significance [of experiences] and one's sensation of them. Incorporated with this is a constant effort and hope to realize a significance in perfect relation to paint.[7]

As he went on with this landscape material, he kept finding possibilities that could be introduced into the composition of the painting which, in a sense, had nothing to do with the particular section of landscape that brought on his emotional reaction. He found he could maintain his emotional state while making a synthesis with landscape material that did not originate in the area of his primary reaction. Very soon he was able to conclude that it was possible to make an organization that was, not as landscape but as painting, structurally strong.

Nature was still there but largely as a source of shapes and their relationships which in themselves he felt to be lacking in something necessary to the painting. Years before he had noted the inadequacy of nature in providing the rhythmic unity which he felt to be requisite in the composition of a painting. He had to introduce that which would carry him from the landscape into and through the painting. Thus we find in the *Earth Rhythms* (Figures 15 and 19) and later in the *Synthesis Series* (Figures 40 and 41) a dominant movement of one kind or another that causes the movement within the landscape element to be picked up and carried along by a rhythmic structure related to painting rather than to landscape.

By a simple division of the area susceptible to many variations and rhythmic activities unlike anything in nature but very right in the painting, he imposed a unifying rhythm that brought coherence to the work. Although the impulse for a painting or a group of paintings had come from something external to the dynamics of painting procedure, the demands of his *unifying principle* necessitated the introduction of factors beyond the initial impulse. A specific point of view developed when Jonson became more interested in exploring his subjective experience with a section of his environment than in a descriptive rendering of that environment.

When the artist tries to paint his sensations as such, his canvas becomes an entity of quite another order than that of a painter representing things. The canvas ceases to be a transparent window looking out at the details of the world. Much of historic painting developed as a deliberate circumvention of the two-dimensional surface. Such conventions as deep-space perspective and modeling served to create the illusion of a window into reality. When artists abandoned these illusionistic conventions, the painting surface asserted itself. The window turned opaque.

The canvas, interposed between the painter and his motif, is an autonomous structure. It cannot be seen through; it has to be worked on. The essence of reality, rather than its description, has to emerge from the painting surface. Now the rhythms, colors, and textures of the painting are meant to be the equivalents of the rhythm, color, and texture of the painter's sensations.

The outcome of Jonson's absorption with the painting as an expression of sensation, rather than as a reflector of environmental appearances, caused him to become more interested in the internal order of his painting than in either his original source of sensation or his subjective expression of it. He became more and more absorbed in the resolution of the rhythmic possibilities lying within his means and eventually began to consider them as ends in themselves.

When this evolution occurred, Jonson experienced a development from an environment-seeing or -feeling person to an environment-creating one.[8]

Years were to pass before Jonson freed himself entirely from the influence of landscape. The natural forms, the perceived rhythms, the local color—all these continued to have their effects, but now his knowledge of them put them under his control. He did with them whatever he chose to do. As late as 1937 he continued to sketch from nature, constantly refreshing himself on that which nature put before him and as constantly rejecting it as the source of subjects which were of themselves important to his painting.

However, another element had entered into the complex of his New Mexico experiences—that of Indian design. Here was a challenge of another sort. Once more confronted by a new stimulus, he felt that possibly he could incorporate into his growing sense of abstraction his reactions to this native art. This type of abstraction, long antedating that of western art, caused him to wonder whether it had a contribution to make to his own kind of abstraction, and whether in one way or another it might become involved in his expanding theory of *design*.

A few works in the early thirties were frankly based on Indian design (see Figure 23). By filtering the Indian design through his own concept of

Figure 23.   *Southwest Arrangement.* 1933. Oil, 45x20 inches.

organization, he was able to make use of it, not by translating it, but rather by adapting it in such a way that it became a factor, soon shorn of its original identity, in the final synthesis of *design.*

Design could thus result by working from the outside through a conception springing from observation. By arrangement, adjustment, additions to, and subtractions from the motifs, a dramatic, dynamic treatment of the subject matter could be set up in such a way that emphasis on organization would be more expressive than emphasis on the subject.

By virtue of its unity, in which color and line, shape and rhythm are each dependent upon and in a sense included in one another, the completed work was to manifest itself as an entity which by its very nature was the embodiment of *design.* It was not an objective in itself; but through *design* all things, both physical and mental, that entered into the work of art could function, both in their individual characters and as the elements of a unity that transcended such characteristics, to fashion a new and, in each work into which *design* in this sense entered, unique statement. Compact organization, exact execution, technical perfection—such things are in themselves evidences of an urge toward an ideal.

13

Abstraction

It has become increasingly clear that Jonson was never attached to subject matter or the description of subject matter as such. Throughout the early and middle years of his development his attempts at defining what he was trying to do were directed to the eventual elimination of the visual aspects of the subject. The outcome of his efforts do not indicate that this was the only result achieved. The meaning of his effort transcends the mere diminution of the subject's presence. The individual work was not related only to specific feelings. The separations that occur, the distinctions that appear, have a great deal more to do with particular experience and with esthetic meaning than they do with the sole drive to emancipate his work from a specific subject. Necessary as it may have been to Jonson's personal growth, the idea of eliminating the appearances of a subject cannot account for or support the meaning of the individual work or the distinctive expression and unique characteristics of a separate series.

The explanation may be connected with several things. From the earliest stages of his attachment to art his concern was with the pictorial image. A good picture resulted from good composition which adjusted and modified the parts for the benefit of the whole. Another factor was Jonson's critical estimate of what his art should be in relation to his expanding, ever more sophisticated, concept of high art. But the more important explanation must be looked for in the complications that are set up within the processes of abstraction.

Jonson produced many fine examples of the abstract during the phase that had to do with work produced from some kind of direct experience. It was one of the richest fields of his creative activity. It is our loss that he did not choose to remain there a while longer, but the field of abstraction as it related to concrete experience was only a way station to something else, even if for a time it was the center of his work.

The alterations in Jonson's painting during the mid twenties initiated more than a decade of productivity through which he was able to accomplish the transition to what he called complete abstraction. The alignment of all the factors necessary to the realization of his hope of achieving pure abstraction occurred at this time. If we understand Jonson's attitude toward his creative processes correctly, this change included not only the ability to produce the look of total abstraction, but also included all the psychic, psychological, and intellectual dispositions and preparations necessary to produce a painting that would be an authentic manifestation of these inner conditions.

When the entire range of Jonson's painting is examined, it should become clear that from the outset his art differentiates itself primarily in degrees and levels of abstraction. Early in his career he wrote:

> One should study nature in two important ways. First and most important by contemplation and getting the feeling of mood and "pattern" mentally so as to have a sure subconscious knowledge of the important elements. Second by drawing patiently all objects, their forms and manner of receiving light. . . .
>
> On this foundation creation may safely be ventured. . . . A thing suggested is better than one definitely drawn out in detail. The more detail one has, the harder the whole is apt to be and illusion has little chance. Nevertheless, one should have the knowledge of detail with the feeling of suggestiveness. The suggestion through knowledge of that which is left out is best.[1]

None of Jonson's representational painting is strictly descriptive, since elements of abstraction are always present. The tendency toward higher abstraction grew in intensity so that his first painting of 1925, after more than a year in which no painting was done, was to a higher degree than ever before abstract—though not, in the estimate of the artist, "pure abstraction." The same can be said of the other major works of that year and the following years.

In the growing realization of his aim, he wrote:

It has been my hope to so purify, simplify, and organize a work that it expresses completely my reaction, or emotion, or sensation in regard to nature, life, and in fact to any object, even to the things that are not visible but have a profound emotional reaction upon one. I feel that it is the inner significance of things that counts and that is a quality that is abstract. It is the abstract that so interests me at present. . . . I believe all emotions, if pure enough, are abstract. Also, all forms exist to us because of an abstract rhythm and design. It is my aim to define them.[2]

In the last half of the twenties Jonson's experience and achievement in the development of his feeling for abstraction had reached such a level of intensity that it precipitated the recognition by him that he had entered into another of the "experiences" which he told about in his talk to the Chili Club:

Santa Fe, 1929. During this year a definite change occurred through a series of specific inspirations with the result most of the work was really abstract. Again a turning point was reached with the accompanying cleansing and feeling of animation.[3]

In following pages many of these works of varying degrees of abstraction will be looked at and discussed and the direct results of the "series of specific inspirations," which Jonson did not specify to his audience, will be examined.

As was earlier noted, Jonson's interest in portraiture largely disappeared after 1920; human figures continued to appear in his work for many years, but usually as a part of the total composition, integrated as contributory shapes and divested of individual personality. However, there are two paintings relating to particular people which, when considered in conjunction with the earlier portraits or characterizations, demonstrate in definite ways the artist's progression toward higher levels of abstraction.

The first of these, *Symphonic Portrait—May Van Dyke* (Plate 2) is a memory portrait, for which the subject did not sit in the usual sense, based on Jonson's feelings and his reactions to his sensations while observing the pianist-composer. It is a concept of a portrait which mingles the seen appearances with the felt emotion in elements of representation and abstraction.

The second work in this demonstration of the development of the abstract is a work done in 1935 titled *Dramatic Figuration* (Figure 24). This painting would be categorized by Jonson as a "pure abstraction" in that there are no items of detail or fact taken from the physical components of the "inspiration" utilized in it. To Ellen Van Volkenburg Browne, who was the "subject of his inspiration," he wrote:

> The painting is an attempt to express in abstract forms and color the amazing sensation and experience of you through realizing some spiritual kinship. For days a kind of happy thrill pervaded this place. I must tell you that you made a beautiful impression on both Vera and myself. In my composition I have hoped to state some of it. I let the thing flow and whatever I have of Nellie in it is intuitive and natural. I hope I have drawn the best portions and that they, in the work, are functional. The work is as abstract as anything can be so I do not suppose anyone but myself will sense the beautiful concept of a great human contact. Even though it is not a "portrait" of you it has resulted because of you and to me that is far greater. I am very happy. . . . I have brought into the visual field in a permanent form the beauty and joy of what I feel to be a mutual understanding of two human beings through the spiritual and the emotional.[4]

In his enthusiasm he also wrote to Maurice Browne:

> It is one of the great emotional contacts of my life. Everything clicked in perfect time and if there ever was a successful mutual understanding through the esthetic, I believe this was one. It isn't often that an abstract rhythm through form can result because of human personality. This time that occurred for I have just done an abstract composition that resulted directly as a result of what Nellie meant to me. It is not a portrait of her but a pure rhythmic composition of a form and design, etc. Of course it may not mean the same thing to anyone else but myself. If so, I do not care for it suffices that at the time I had the great emotion and felt right and consistent in the order I was establishing.[5]

Figure 24.   *Dramatic Figuration*. 1935. Oil, 32x24 inches.

14

Developments

There is a painting from 1926, *Spring (Seasons Series)* (Figure 25), which is of an entirely different character than the landscape around Santa Fe concerning which Jonson wrote, "This country is cold and bare with wide open spaces as well as the mountains. It is not the South. There is nothing languorous about the place. The altitude is too high for that. There is not a profusion of growth. In fact, here is the material for starkness."[1]

Spring is a departure from this far less than lush quality of the New Mexican landscape. In Chicago in 1922, a short time after finishing *Winter*, Jonson had made an attempt to add *Spring* to the series. Concerning that attempt, he wrote in his diary, "For about two weeks I've been working on composition *Spring*. Began it some time ago. Have worked sincerely on it and have in sincerity and disgust destroyed it all, entirely. All wrong—sweet."[2]

Four years later, after his move to Santa Fe, Jonson came back to the subject and produced the painting we know.

In it there is a burgeoning of earth, an upward thrust of growth, a revitalizing of color that stands in contrast to other works of its year. There is an exuberance of shapes ranging from those of almost realistic plant renderings to abstractions and symbols invented to summon the spirit of the subject season. Human bodies, plant life, and earth forms contribute shapes that are assembled into coherence to express the oneness of nature which finds further emphasis in the unity-in-diversity of the painting as a whole. A springtime atmosphere bathes the scene. All is happiness. One feels with the artist the vernal rapture.

Figure 25. *Spring (Seasons Series)*. 1926. Oil, 41x28 inches.

Every aspect of this painting is in sharp contrast with the symbolic import of its forerunner, *Winter*. Like *Winter*, it is a landmark work. Although Jonson had previously painted trees, *Spring* has little in common with the earlier paintings. Its use of color and its different attitude toward landscape led to the eight *Growth Variants* (1929–35).

The *Growth Variants* (Figures 26 and 27) were not simple extensions of the treatment found in *Spring*. Though they also were expositions of plant forms, they were generally more abstract and branched out into a wide catalog of growth patterns. A change in rhythmic characteristics was brought to the abstracted motifs of trees and plant forms.

The *Growth Variants* helped liberate Jonson from the earth-sky format so fundamental and dominating in his landscape paintings. Shapes breeze through the painting space in free and arbitrary ways that yet fall under the control of his emotional demand for a formal order. Of more importance is the color pitch. There is a translucence, as though the forms have depth in which light sinks and then floats back to the eye. For a painter who constantly exclaimed about brilliant color, the various earth-derived paintings tend to be heavy, dense, and shadowed beside the emerging, brighter tonalities of the *Growth Variants*.

In addition to the first five of the *Growth Variants*, 1929 saw the beginning of the *Digits* series (1929–30). The ten paintings of the digits, represented in the Retrospective Collection by *Abstract Four* (Figure 28) and *Abstract Five*, are developments of the conventional symbols representing the numbers. The painter probably picked them as subjects because they were "cool" material, that is, as subjects they did not come out of a reactive emotion and therefore offered the possibility of freer action in reference to invention and organization of the painting.

Each digit is also developed as an abstraction of the human figure, which adds to its complexity. In these small, tightly knit works there is a play between lyrical and dramatic elements woven into a unity. The group has an additional interesting step in that color is a specific part of the subject matter, since each of the ten digits is assigned a particular color emphasis. From this point on, color functions in Jonson's work as an independent expressive force which, nevertheless, is still embedded in the unity demanded by *design*.

For the artist the paintings of the digits held importance in that he felt

Figure 26. *Growth Variant No. I.* 1929. Oil, 38x27 inches.

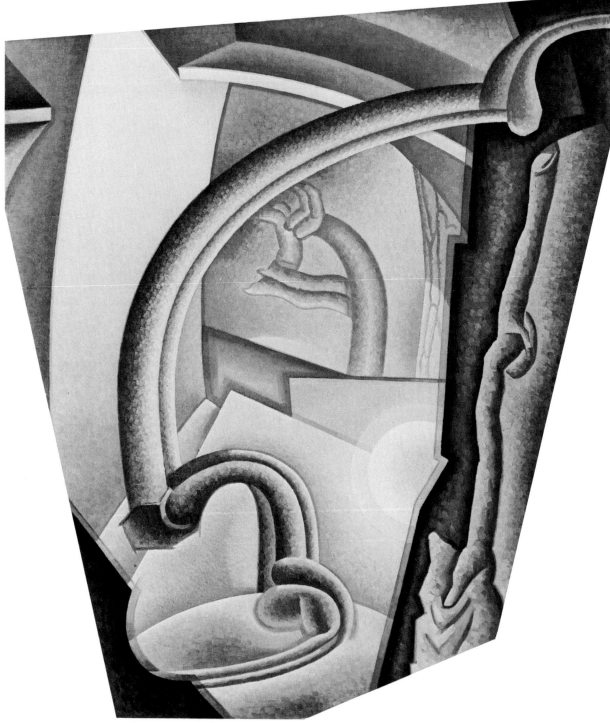

Figure 27. *Growth Variant No. VII.* 1931.
Oil, 35x30 inches, irregular.

Figure 28. *Abstract Four.* 1929. Oil, 24x15 inches.

he had achieved "real" abstraction of a sort that, although it was in part based on objective materials, was very close to freedom from the demands of such subject matter. Concerning them he wrote:

> There is the group of abstract organizations which mean more to me than anything done to date. Here I believe I have or am touching on an approach to realization. But the birth pangs are at times terrific. . . . Isn't it amazing what variations of all the elements are possible when once one has felt? Rhythm with guts—color with life—form that moves with a thunderclap and feeling with all the subtle items present are the things in a work of art. . . . There is no limit.[3]

The successful exploration of the *Digits* suggested a comparable use of the letters of the alphabet. In 1930 the first of the twenty-six *Variations on a Rhythm* (1930–36) was painted (see Figures 29 and 30).

In this series it is the rhythmic force evolved from the shapes of the letters that is the "subject matter." The basic rhythms are carried out in echoes and counter rhythms using abstract shapes which, one surmises, involve memories of nature, though it is unnecessary and perhaps unwise to seek such references in the paintings, for the shapes exist only to enforce the rhythms postulated by the titles. As in the paintings of the digits, the *Variations on a Rhythm* establish their own different note in the use of color. In this case there is a shifting from the mellow and deep tones of the various landscape paintings with their dramatic dark and light values to color keys that are more richly endowed with chromatic effects.

Another set of five paintings, 1930–33, *Abstraction in Blue, in Yellow, in Red, in Green,* and *in Violet* provided Jonson with further proof that the subject of his work could be provided by an element of his medium. Of this series, *Abstraction in Blue* and *Abstraction in Red* (Plate 3) remain in the Retrospective Collection. Of the latter, Jonson wrote:

> This work is the result of an effort to express the emotional meaning of the color RED through an abstract design. The forms and the resulting design are entirely creative in that they appear because of the concept of an abstract order through emotional realization. Some of the items that presented themselves at the

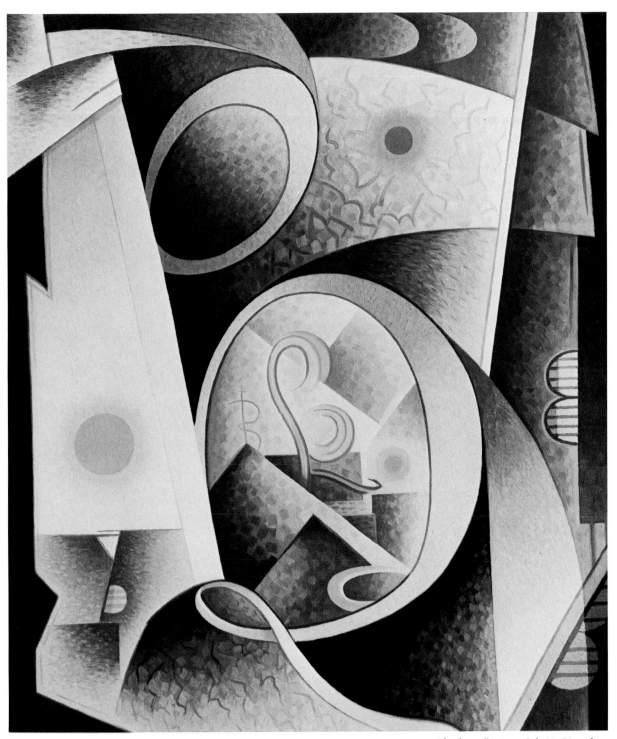

Figure 29.   *Variations on a Rhythm—B.* 1931. Oil, 33x29 inches.

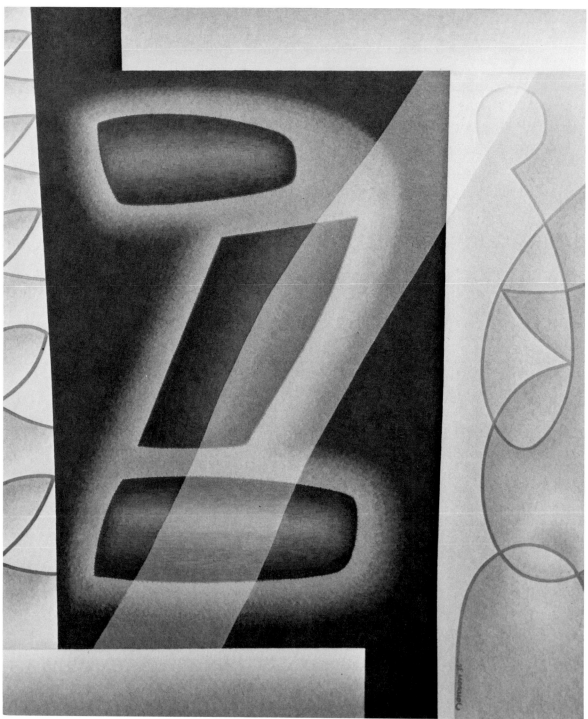

Figure 30.   *Variations on a Rhythm—Z.* 1936. Oil, 38x33 inches.

time are: an insistence of red—a thrust of force—an interweaving of three dimensional forms with two dimensional transparent planes.[4]

The *Digits*, the *Variations on a Rhythm*, and the color abstractions were conceptually and in their assemblage of shapes almost a complete break with nature. Jonson was tremendously excited. Here was a way of abstraction in which landscape, still life, and the human figure were unnecessary. True, they were all ingredients, but they were not the stimulus nor were they necessary in the final resolution. The letters and numbers are conventional symbols which by themselves, out of context, connote very little, if any, emotional substance. Consequently, what is done with them in developing a type of painting organization is of the utmost importance. Working with them, Jonson was able to sustain his thrust toward purification.

A major change took place in his entire outlook when, through these groups of works, he realized that he could progress on to painting released from any representational inclusions whatever:

> At times I do get a glimpse of meaning to it all and then the whole world is rosy until the effort to express it proves a failure. Art is not the business of making pictures. That is simple. It is rather something like creating a new rhythm, a new reality. It becomes a struggle to express some universal law as we find it in life and nature. A sensation and a feeling are mighty fundamental and illusive things. And this is only part of it. . . .[5]

In work after work Jonson could visualize the necessary setup. The *design* factor functioned in such a way that his excitement came from a mental vision of a created order, a created balance, a created harmony.

A number of questions presented themselves: Cannot a totally nonrepresentational art be a stronger affair, a richer organization, than the assemblage of a great deal of material which is related to nature rather than to painting? Is it possible to extend the whole creative gesture into a deeper, larger, richer field and give greater emotional impact? Cannot pure design be developed into an organization which will stimulate a rich response because it is a more immediate, direct, and intimate type of experience?

In trying to answer these questions Jonson had to get at the problems of creating form from the elements fundamental to painting itself. He had to learn to do this without introducing matters extraneous to painting, and he had to approach his work with an emotional clarity attuned to his concept of an absolute, created art.

Thus he was approaching closer to his goal of an art free from subject matter other than that inherent in the elements and materials of painting and how they are influenced by the thoughts and feelings of the artist. This was the art that Kandinsky had called "absolute," a term adopted by Jonson, a nondescriptive, nonobjective art because there were no natural objects in existence from which it had been abstracted.

15

New York and Chicago

During the winter of 1931–32 Jonson was in New York, not only to mount his exhibition at the Delphic Studios, but also to experience the city in its cultural aspects. Vera remained behind in Santa Fe and after two months joined him in New York. In the interim he wrote many letters to her, and excerpts from them serve to give a brief summary of his experience:

> I have moved in for I rented the place at 13 East 14th. It's a messy place but I believe I can make it at least decent. Well, it's going to be a bohemian studio all right but as I do not care for that sort of thing it will, I fear, lose its value for me. I have moved in and this is what it amounts to.

> New York is a madhouse but perhaps I feel it so much because I am not settled. I have been busy every minute and most of the nights. I have seen, I suppose, 150 people. So altogether it has been hectic. At times I wish very strongly you were here. And I feel now that Santa Fe will look mighty good at the expiration of the six months set for the New York experience.

> Yesterday at a musical tea a piano sonata of [Roy Harris] was played and played beautifully. My God, what modern music. Really, I have the feeling it is the best thing. . . . it certainly is the most important thing I have heard or seen since arriving. There it is—when painting becomes as pure a medium we can perhaps paint pure emotion with all the trimmings of form—life—love, etc. . . . Yes, if I can reach some means to say plastically what music says in sound I shall have done something besides express my personal reactions.

Life is the great thing—an inner and outer life, I believe, can make for an undying beauty. And you know so well my belief in and of beauty. Art is the great key to life for it encompasses everything. That is, my concept of art. Life is art and art is life.

Perhaps in the offing lies the great material for work that I have spoken of and have never realized in form. Surely optical seeing is not that material expressing the essence of life and thought and feeling. Is it not rather an inner seeing?

Tomorrow the Matisse show opens at the Modern Museum. That and my own will be two exciting affairs here this season anyhow. I think the Marin exhibit important but after all it is not the supreme kind of emotion that I believe is possible in paint. But the more I see the more faith have I in the greatness of the great abstract. And as yet I have not seen one great abstract work.

We have attended some exhibitions. The finest was the Juan Gris at the Harriman Gallery. Oh! what beautiful works. I do not see how anyone can see such work and not realize that in painting lies a great salvation and the possibility of pure beauty.

I went to the formal opening of the Whitney Museum of Art. It was a grand affair. And what a place! But the canvases, numbering 210 I believe, which are hung are not so much. The canvas that meant the most to me that day and which has carried over as a very important and beautiful work is Demuth's *My Egypt*. It is the finest work by an American I have seen.

It has happened in seeing painting! One of the finest and certainly most unusual experiences has come to me in seeing painting. Of such beauty and of such emotion that I must write you immediately. Modigliani! A whole exhibition in retrospect, beautifully presented and of terrific importance. For the first time I have actually wept as a result of [an] emotional experience from painting. After seeing everything, I saw in the center on a table Modigliani's death mask and with that the whole effort opened up and it was as if the entire significance flooded down upon me and I could not help but cry. I feel like one who has seen a new significance to life. It is the same but it is emphasized.

Our final quotation from these letters, a statement of substantial worth resulting from his varied experiences in New York, sums up the virtual totality of Jonson's concept of art:

> I believe in the art—emotion—and love idea of the universe in which we find ourselves. I cannot but feel our subconscious is held within the physical world. I believe in life and I love life and I want all I can get of it and in so doing I live. And what I leave behind after I am through with it is not to be some unknown, unsolved riddle of the esoteric idea or some mystical idea of creation but rather a rich message for man of man because it includes all thoughts and ideas possible within the mind of man. That in a sense is the real meaning of the abstract in art. So you see I do not throw anything overboard because all thoughts and activities are a part of man and one should not bind oneself to one particular concept or *idée fixe* but take in, emotionally, all things and from it select and if one is in tune the subconscious will make its choice too.[1]

Among the results of Jonson's stay in New York were emotional refreshment and a reappraisal of his own direction. Another immediate result was to confirm himself in his decision to live and work in New Mexico.

The painting result of the stay was a group of seven canvases completed after his return to Santa Fe (see Figure 31). They came at a time when his interest in objective subject matter as a source of abstraction was on the wane. At a time comparable to the period of the *Earth Rhythms* there might have been a city rhythms series, but this was not to be. When his imagination took hold of the theme it did not go toward the power and directness of abstraction as exemplified in other contemporaneous works but worked itself out in paintings touched with fantasy. These paintings express the ideal of the Futurist dreamers who thought the city should be "Huge, tumultuous, agile, mobile, dynamic in all parts, like a gigantic machine. . . ."[2]

In January of 1932 Jonson left New York for Chicago. There, at the Studio Gallery of Increase Robinson, an exhibition of the works shown at the

Figure 31.   *City Perspectives (Second Version)*. 1933.
Oil, 48x38 inches.

Delphic Studio (enhanced by an additional dozen oils, four watercolors, and six drawings) opened on the eighth of the month.

Jonson's visit to Chicago was an opportunity to renew old contacts, and he was well remembered for his activities there a decade earlier. The *Chicago Evening Post* headlined its article "An Art Rebel Revisits His Battle Fields," and went on to say:

> Raymond Jonson, pioneer modern artist, and one of the instigators of the "bloodless" Chicago art revolution of a decade ago, returned last week to the scene of the early struggles of modern art for recognition here.
>
> Seven years ago, when Jonson left Chicago for Santa Fe, the name of Matisse was still enough to frighten little children away from cookie jars. Today, back with a show of his own at the Studio Gallery Increase Robinson in Diana court, Jonson finds even the goblin Picasso shorn of much of his hideousness. . . .
>
> Things weren't so tranquil in the years just following the war when Jonson and Weisenborn and Carl Hoeckner and a few other progressives were rebelling against art conditions in Chicago. At that time the czars of conservatism were in control at the Art Institute. Regularly the modern artists sent in their work to the American show jury. Regularly it was rejected. . . . Jonson and his colleagues at last resorted to open mutiny. One year they organized a "salon of the rejected" . . . and people going back and forth between the two shows began to talk and compare them. Out of this first open rebellion grew the no-jury exhibitions of subsequent years. The tide of independence was rising. . . . Now, after seven years, Jonson has returned to Chicago to find the currents of art flowing comparatively freely through the yearly exhibits at the institute.[3]

A gentle and peaceful man, Jonson had not sought out the role of a "rebel." Conflict violated his sense of rightness and order. But he did believe firmly in the right of the creative life and its products to exist and to be seen as well as the shoddy products of a commercial world. For that right he was willing to instigate a rebellion against "the czars of conservatism."

Among his many activities during his 1932 visit to Chicago was a visit to the University of Chicago where he saw and was impressed by a group of string constructions and sculpturesque forms derived from mathematical equations. Again in 1933, when he was in Chicago for the Century of Progress Exposition, he visited the Hall of Science. When he there again saw these mathematically derived constructions, he was thrilled and began to speculate on the possibilities of making use of items of that nature in his own work. This was the germ which eventuated in *A Cycle of Science* (Figures 32 and 33).

The early thirties saw the beginnings and development of the Great Depression. Jonson noted with misgivings what he felt was a downgrading effect of the depression on the world of art and wrote:

> The depression that has hit the world will produce some grand examples of pot-boilers. . . . Does it matter? Only that what little respect there is [for art] will probably be shot to pieces. Painting as an art will be trampled on. There is going to be a great revival of so-called great art—murals which will now again be called frescos. Grand illustrations to advertise some other activity. Education on a grand scale. We will have art even if it is necessary to manufacture it. We will make a business out of it all. All of which counts for nothing compared to one great work. So I wash my hands of it all, except the true work.[4]

Later on, he continued in the same vein:

> I am disturbed over the terrible mess in regard to the attitude toward what the artist should paint. The painters seem to have lost track of the real reason for painting. Certainly it is not to please the purchaser nor for a means to earn a living. I always thought it was for the purpose of feeding the soul. I have not heard of one real justification for placing art on a footing with business and politics. . . . In the long run it does not matter for the real workers are hidden away working. Some may be starving along with it but some of us will manage to do some labor independent of attempting to combine the two. Of course, I realize each case is an individual one. And I also think it should remain so especially when concerned with the world of the spirit rather than the physical.[5]

During the decade of the depression there was an absurdly overpublicized emphasis on a small group of painters who continually reached the press with anti–modern art propaganda. Some of them had returned from Europe disillusioned by what they had seen there and probably with a poor understanding of its implications. At home they fostered an emphasis on nationalism and a return to descriptive painting. One of their champions, an eminent critic of the period, purveyed this sentiment thus: "Art for its own sake, or beauty's sake, or for the sake of any abstraction whatever will not thrive in America. It means the kind of painting exhibited by our international dealers is a hothouse product nurtured in little pots of imported soil, and that it will never exert an iota of influence in American life or thought. It means that if we are ever to have an indigenous expression, it will be an art proceeding from strong native impulses, simple ideas and popular tastes. . . ."[6]

The notion of a group of flag-waving American artists rejecting the creative thought of the artistic world and dedicating themselves to the sights and the interpretation of their native land held an enormous appeal to a wide section of the American public.

Jonson's reaction to this situation was vigorous:

> I happen to be an American and wish to remain so. But my intention is that in being so I am also an international or universal. Now it happens that I am not interested in telling the farmer and the politician about our country but rather in telling about the wonders of a richer, deeper land—the world of peace-loving and human emotions projected through pure form. . . . I will not budge one fraction away from what I feel and know.[7]

An overwhelming reality of the thirties was poverty. Artists who were normally adjusted to living on its fringes, as Jonson was, were pinched even harder by the drying up of what little economic support had been available to them. Realizing that artists are subject to hunger and cold like others among the unemployed, both state and federal governments developed art projects as a form of work relief.

Among the institutions that indicated an interest in cooperating with the efforts of the Public Works Art Project, initiated in 1933, was the

University of New Mexico. Offering the walls of its library, the university asked that Jonson be assigned to the project. Hence, along with Willard Nash, Jonson was proffered the opportunity to provide paintings to decorate the library. Since no competition was involved, he felt that he could accept the offer, particularly since it seemed to him that, in all of the commissions of which he was aware, there was no abstract work. He felt there should be at least one painter whose work would be abstract or at least semiabstract. There was the further inducement that he would have complete freedom of choice as to subject matter and would also be free of supervision and direction in all phases of the execution of the works.

The memory of his visit to the Hall of Science at the Century of Progress Exposition was fresh in his memory. The mathematical constructions which had fascinated him seemed an appropriate starting point for decorating the library of an educational institution. The result was *A Cycle of Science* (Figures 32 and 33).

The cycle consists of six works—*Mathematics* (35 x 45 inches), *Biology* (85 x 55 inches), *Astronomy* (60 x 105 inches), *Engineering* (60 x 70 inches),

Figure 32. *A Cycle of Science—Mathematics*. 1934. Oil, 35x45 inches.

Figure 33. *A Cycle of Science—Chemistry.* 1934.
Oil, 80x37 inches. Photographer unknown.

Chemistry (80 x 37 inches), and *Physics* (80 x 37 inches)—to fit the wall spaces assigned to him. Eventually, the library was converted to other uses. Fortunately, the paintings were not irretrievably attached to the walls, so they were removed from the building and are now part of the Retrospective Collection at Jonson Gallery. Chronologically, the six works were done between the first of the *City Series* in 1933 and the last in 1936 and concluded his use of this type of subject matter.

Concerning *A Cycle of Science,* Jonson wrote:

> My aim and hope in these works has been to present a series of compositions that expresses my emotional concept of a plastic idea based on the particular subjects that came to mind. Also I feel my plan presents the idea that contemporary knowledge offers an emotional and spiritual approach. . . . .
>
> It has been my hope to create works that are esthetically significant executed in such a manner that they will take their proper position in space on the wall and be related artistically in their environment.
>
> Each composition is the result of a definite concept of a color harmony in relation to the form and design. I think of them as symphonic compositions consistent with my medium and honest to the highest ideal I stand for.[8]

These six paintings, together with those of another commission under the WPA/FAP (similarly free of supervision or interference in choice of subject matter and manner of execution), fulfilled Jonson's hope that somewhere in the jungle of federally sponsored art there should be works that were abstract.[9] The second commission was for a pair of works, each 60 x 90 inches, titled *Science* and *Art,* installed at Eastern New Mexico University in Portales.

Thus his visits to New York and Chicago in the early thirties resulted not only in the series of city paintings but also in the eight commissioned works which served as a virtual consummation of Jonson's work with abstractions derived from the landscape and other material sources, for within the period of their completion he was on the threshold of total nonrepresentation derived from the inner sources of instinct, feeling, and creative thought.

16

Trilogies and Cycles

Prominent in the collection Jonson took to New York for his exhibition were two trilogies, the *Grand Canyon Trilogy* (1927) (Figure 34) and *Time Cycle—Morning, Noon, Night* (1930) (Figure 35).

We have seen that Jonson was a painter who tended to produce works in series of more or less closely related works such as the aforementioned *Seasons Series, The Digits,* and others. But there were also sets so closely related that they were conceived of as a single work. These were the trilogies, cycles, and a few other sets variously titled. Experiencing these groups is alone worth the examination of the Retrospective Collection.

A visit to the Grand Canyon in 1927 developed into a strong emotional experience.[1] Jonson felt that his canyon sketches had to be used to record, to give expression to this experience. Considering the scope of the material, the excitement of the encounter, and the compulsion to express what had been seen and felt, he concluded that a single painting, however large, could not do justice to the subject. Consequently, the multiple format was adopted, and so the trilogy concept was born. The *Grand Canyon Trilogy,* whose combined width is thirteen and a half feet, is a monumental work about a monumental fact of nature and the monumental feelings it had evoked.

In his enthusiasm over the entire episode, Jonson decided that he would paint a series of such works, each based on a major natural phenomenon capable of arousing comparable reactions. Hence in 1928 he painted the *Carlsbad Caverns Trilogy,* based, like its predecessor, on drawings made at the site.

Eight years were to pass before the appearance of another trilogy. In the interim he had largely discarded his interest in the representation, however abstract, of nature. The ambitious program he had visualized no longer attracted him. Consequently, the *Spiral Trilogy* of 1936 had nothing to do with the type of subject matter of the first two trilogies and everything to do with painting. Nonrepresentational, it deals primarily with the shape of a spiral, and the three paintings examine some of the mutations to which that shape may be subjected by an artist.

Generally, each of the trilogies that followed at irregular intervals falls into a similar category and is typical of the kind of work being done at the time of execution. Knowledge of the trilogies supplies a synoptic knowledge of what Jonson was doing over a long span of his painting experience.

The Retrospective Collection contains sixteen trilogies, six cycles, seven pairs, a triptych (1966), and three other coordinated sets: *A Cycle of Science* (six 1934 oils), *Improvisations Set in a Structure—Five Variations* (1958), and *Development of a Frustration in Four Stages* (1961).

A listing of the trilogies in the Retrospective Collection indicates the variety of concepts which entered into these works.

1927	Grand Canyon Trilogy
1928	Carlsbad Caverns Trilogy
1936	Spiral Trilogy
1940	Trilogy—Evolution
1940	Esoteric Trilogy
1943	Trilogy—Tension
1943	Trilogy—Dissonance
1944	Trilogy—Dynamics
1945	Surrealist Trilogy
1945	Trilogy—Continuous Movement
1948	Variations on a Linear Theme—A Trilogy
1949	Miniature Trilogy
1954	Primary Directions Trilogy
1958	Red, White, and Blue Trilogy
1966	Light—A Trilogy
1973	Suspended Shapes in Open Support—Trilogy[2]

Figure 34. *Grand Canyon Trilogy.* 1927.
Three oils, 45x56 inches, 67½x52½x9 inches, 45x56 inches.

In 1930 Jonson painted the first of his cycles. It is also a trilogy, like all but one of the six cycles, but the intention in these works is not the same as in the trilogies. As he came to 1930, Jonson realized that he had come to a parting of the ways in his work and decided to sum up the past in a *Time Cycle* (Figure 35) which was intended as a type of farewell to reliance on representation. The cycles have appeared at ten-year intervals since the first with the exception of the most recent. The cycles are:

1930   Time Cycle
1940   Life Cycle
1950   Space Cycle
1960   Color Cycle (four works)
1970   Curvilinear Cycle
1973   "1980"—Symmetrical-Geometrical Cycle

The titles alone indicate that, unlike the first of them, the other cycles are not so much summations of time periods of work as of the kind of painting subjects that interested him, hence space, color, and shapes. An exception was the *Life Cycle,* which brought into being a concept that had been in Jonson's consciousness for at least twenty years. He wanted to express in paint the relationships of male and female, the sexual quotient in life, and in 1940 he achieved his purpose. He invented or adapted various phallic symbols with which to work and built them into three powerful and brilliantly colorful casein tempera paintings.

In the first of the cycles, *Time Cycle—Morning, Noon, Night* (Figure 35), Jonson was working with symbols, as had frequently been the case in previous years. Basic to the design are three directional devices. *Morning* establishes a diagonal to the right upward; *Noon,* a vertical; *Night* a diagonal to the right downward. These primary directions are reinforced by a coordinated tonal color scheme expressive of the time elements.

C. J. Bulliet described the *Time Cycle* in this way:

In *Morning, Noon,* and *Night* he works out most amazingly the mystical significance of the time of day by the use of conic sections—those that go off into infinity for the dawn, those that close tight for noon, and those that round off to an elliptical consummation at evening.[3]

Figure 35. *Time Cycle.* 1930. Oils.
Morning, 33x38 inches; *Noon*, 36x38 inches; *Night*, 33x38 inches.

The three paintings are abstractions, not quite as geometrical as Bulliet implied, involving discernible, though abstracted, natural shapes and forms. The sun—rising, at high noon, and setting—is one element. Another consists of saplings that develop into mature trees and on to gnarled and broken old age. In the first canvas mists coalesce into clouds over mountain shapes. In the light of noon the clouds are dispersed, the mountains are sternly synthesized, and there is a sensation of pause and equilibrium. Finally, with the approach of night the clouds become beautifully conceived dreamlike shapes hovering over the sleeping earth.

"The mystical significance of the time of day" may well be present, but it is doubtful that Jonson was dealing in any mysticism other than the ever-present mystery that time and space have always been to people as they confronted them.

This description of the *Time Cycle* is to a degree a description of the general nature of the trilogies and the cycles in that they declare a theme with variations.

In 1973 by painting *"1980"—Symmetrical-Geometrical Cycle* Jonson broke the rhythm of the cycles appearing at intervals of a decade. He had expressed to the writer the thought that because of the limitations of his lifetime there might not be a cycle following that of 1970. The writer countered with the observation that an artist need not be time bound; the future remains open to the imagination, and an imaginative development could appear through the contemplation and projection of the hopes and aspirations one might hold for the future. As this could be the basis for another interesting advancement, the writer suggested a "future series" to counteract the thought of the limitations of mortality. Jonson mulled this thought over and as a result painted a "1980" cycle.

17

The Spiritual in Art

During the thirties, when regionalism was dominating American art, Jonson continued in his own direction. In this decade he was able to define his concepts and give them logical expression:

> In the realms of pure organization there is the vehicle for great emotional expression and reaction. By pure organization I mean abstract [nonrepresentational]. To make of this a sure and real vehicle is another struggle. What I want and expect to get is a form that will function as nicely in color as music. I believe color to be as great a medium as sound, as color contains within it all the possible means to great composition.

> [A painting] in itself is something and is the only thing of its kind. Some of us want to do the same thing with color, line, and shape that the musician can do with sound. We want to compose independent of imitation and to express in plastic form the inner significance of vibrations and a certain sense of cosmic rightness through the functioning of the intellect and the subconscious.

> The function of the artist is to create or present something that is a statement of the finest qualities conceivable in the human mind and emotions.[1]

> The more I work the more satisfying it becomes in that I feel I am able to see into the plastic meaning of a concept in the direction of composition and space and light as well as the thrill of

actually making something that can stand on its own two feet as it were. Then too, I want to feel that by working I can state those fundamental rhythms of life that are constructive and basically permanent. Art is for carrying over the individualistic meaning of life.[2]

[Also] art's office is the creation of a unity. It is concerned in discovering and setting forth the wonders of a natural world with the wonder of the other—the human intellect. It is concerned in bringing about the fusion of matter with spirit, which is the object of creation itself.[3]

Later, in a talk to the Chili Club, Jonson said:

I believe that the truest and best of our *design* in painting is sophisticated and sacred. I call it sacred because with this creative use of *design* a spiritual height can be attained.[4]

By "sophisticated" Jonson meant the apex of an historical process with the fullest and most dynamic use of all the means pertinent to painting in significant relationship to the artist's intention. As for the sacred quality which he posited, we may find a shadow of its meaning in such definitions as are to be found in Whitehead's "vision of something which stands beyond, behind and within the passing flux of immediate things; something which is real, and yet waiting to be realized; something which is a remote possibility, and yet the greatest of present facts; something which gives meaning to all that passes, and yet eludes apprehension; something whose possession is the final good, and yet is beyond all reach; something which is the ultimate ideal, and the hopeless quest."[5]

Jonson did not believe the sacred to be "beyond all reach" nor did he believe it to be "the hopeless quest." He believed that art is precisely the vehicle by which is expressed the otherwise inexpressible, and he proceeded on that basis.

18

Absolute Art

In a series of watercolors termed *Arabesques* (Figure 36) the look of free invention is such that the abstraction may be called total. In the same year as the first *Arabesques* were painted, 1933, Jonson produced a group of twenty-six pencil drawings of a high degree of abstraction. Some of these drawings, such as *Ascending Circle* (Figure 37), go beyond abstraction to such an extent that they look entirely nonrepresentational.

Another series of paintings, titled *Figurations,* was begun in 1934. They extended Jonson's research along his creative direction farther into the resources native to painting. Although they advanced him along the path toward nonobjective, emotionally free painting, they exemplify something of utmost importance to the appreciation of Jonson's work. This small group, although considered a series, typifies the breadth of his personal approach to the creation of works that attempt to bring into focus an emotional concept. In their variety—contrast *Dramatic Figuration* (Figure 24) with *Prismatic Figuration* (Plate 4)—they show how he has taken into account the full complexity and depth of mind and feeling. Each work finds the abstract level distinctive to itself. In each he has translated feeling into the particular forms that best reveal the force of his concept. The paintings encourage viewers to associate themselves with the feeling implicit in freely formed lines and their subsequent shapes and spaces. One must note that the color in each work strikes an individual chord to establish, while liberating, its particular mood.

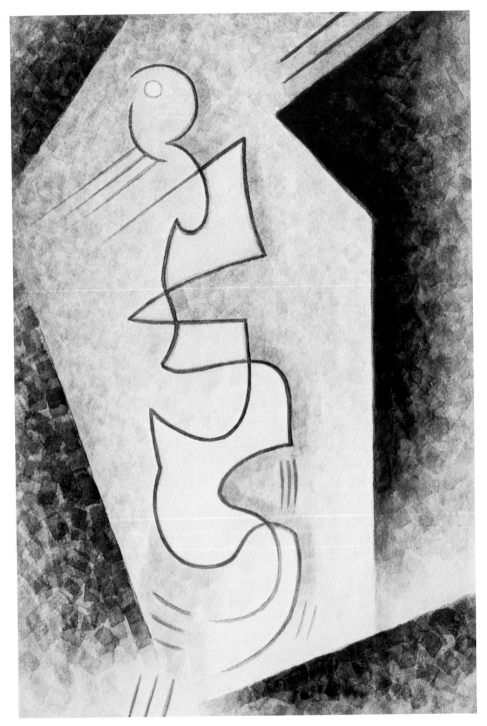

Figure 36.   *Arabesque No. 1.* 1933. Watercolor, 19x13 inches.

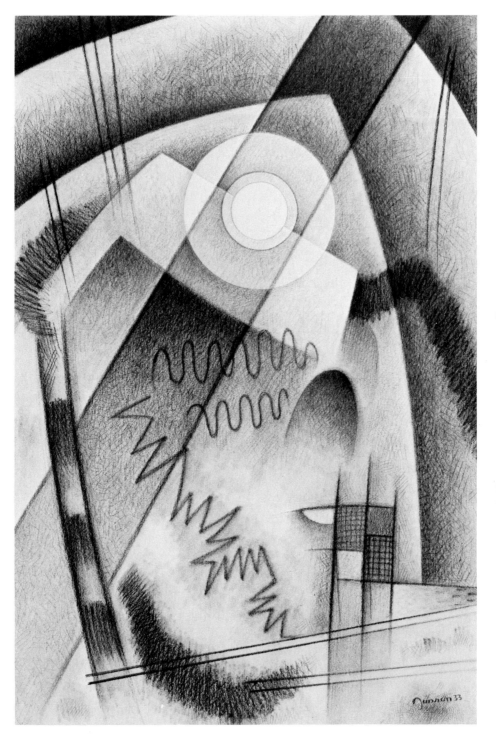

Figure 37. *Ascending Circle.* 1933. Pencil drawing, 19x13 inches.

In the midst of all this painting 1936 saw another group of abstract drawings. Some of them have a symbolic significance, others seem related, often remotely, to nature—if not to the landscape itself, surely to the artist's reaction to landscape forms. Highlighting this group of drawings is a series of six *Dramatic Forms* of which No. 3 (Figure 38), the only one in the Retrospective Collection, is reproduced here to give the savor of these handsome works.

The nine oils of the *Figuration* series were followed by a related, though different in general appearance, series of seven watercolors and one oil called *Interlocked Forms* (Figure 39) in which "the memory of nature" seems to have been eliminated entirely.

The first painted in 1934 and the last in 1947, the paintings of the *Synthesis* series (Figures 40 and 41) are sixteen in number. The works demonstrate how strongly Jonson believed in letting the subconscious function. When it did so to bring forward feelings and memories of the forms of nature he had so intently studied, he accepted this presence as part of the natural, instinctive route he was trying to travel. From time to time, whenever the forms of nature were recognized as still entering into his painting, he apparently accepted the challenge and turned it in the direction of his intention, purging as well as expressing the influence. The *Synthesis* (Figures 40 and 41) series is a part of the momentum toward the purification of his painting. These works seem to be an extension of the *Earth Rhythms* (Figures 15 and 19) more fully abstracted, with the power of the *design* thesis more fully extended. Freely devised forms and landscape elements "in perfect relation to paint"[1] meet within an invented organization.

Of a different order, the *Universe Series*, begun in 1935, and the *Cosmic Theme* series (Figure 42), started in 1936, indicate that Jonson was indeed achieving a release from landlocked concepts. Long earthbound, the artist leaps into the cosmos. Rhythms develop in any and all directions. The paintings are open, airy, mysterious. Jonson wrote:

> In regard to *Cosmic Theme No. Three,* it is primarily structural and not in any way naturalistic or imitative. Rhythm is an important attribute and in a sense the composition is built in relationship to an emotional comprehension of the kind of rhythm pertaining to the movement of spheres in space. In regard to space the intention

Figure 38.   *Dramatic Forms No. 3.* 1936.
Crayon drawing, 19x26 inches.

Figure 39.   *Interlocked Forms—Suspension.* 1937.
Watercolor, 20x33 inches.

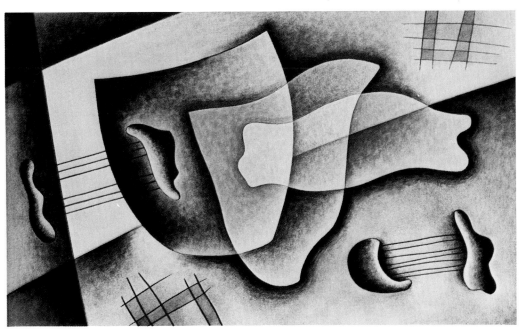

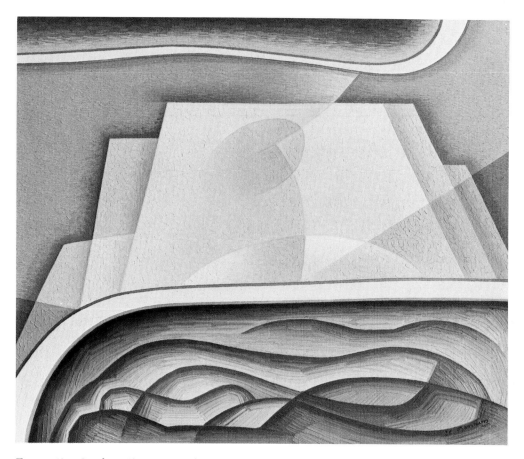

Figure 40. *Synthesis Five*. 1936. Oil, 22x27 inches.

has been to create a painting space and not a realistic one. I believe one might interpret certain items as symbolic, such as the interplay between the many circles or transparent spheres, and the curvilinear shapes. Do they not suggest ethereal material in space in the act of becoming formed into matter? The color possesses an interesting interplay because of the great degree of transparency . . . with an overall effect of light and luminosity.[2]

There are few better examples of the use of transparency than *Cosmic Theme No. Three* (Figure 42). The device of transparency conveys supremely the interpenetration of things. By merging and transmuting shapes and colors beneath elusive veils, the artist makes each shape and color truly

Figure 41. *Synthesis Fourteen (Oil No. 11—1947)*. 45x35 inches.

Figure 42. *Cosmic Theme No. Three.* 1937. Oil, 28x40 inches.

become part of the other, and we are made to feel the universe growing before us. What makes the visionary world so real is that whatever is indefinite and fantastic is firmly juxtaposed with the concrete and with the logic of planes, surfaces, textures, and rational transitions.

Transparency demonstrates the use of a technical item that can bring the viewer an intensification of feeling and a stimulation of the imagination. It became a continuing, insistent, and beautiful element in Jonson's work over a long span of years. It has been utilized as a device to enhance color and to cause form to emerge into a different kind of unfixed illusionary space. In setting up multiple planes to produce the look of transparency the artist achieves the appearance of varying degrees of shallow and deep space while remaining true to the surface plane of the canvas. Transitions of color and value can be made from one created plane to another without violating the real primary surface. The illusion of transparency becomes the means for close modifications of harmonies as well as surprising juxtapositions of color in unexpected spatial situations. Where transparencies are used in Jonson's oil paintings, color and surface take on a quality of richness unlike that in any of his other works in that medium. In watercolor after watercolor, as in the oils, transparency releases color from weight, light from substance, and provides a transcendental sensation that the artist and viewer alike can define as spiritual.

By the late thirties Jonson had achieved a considerable body of works to which he felt he could apply the word "absolute," in the sense that the word is used in the phrase "absolute music," and in which the *design* concept had come to a complete realization. He felt that he had developed a visual organization which eliminated sensations related to any type of external, objective experience. He summed up the attitude which had produced such fruition:

> The hope has been to arrive at a state of pure feeling; to create through the spirit rather than the physical; to deal with shapes, forms and color in such a way that they appear to expose the spirit of man rather than his physical being; to go beyond the appearance of the world and its forms into a realm of idealistic condition of order and space that pertains to structure as it can function in the plastic creative act. Some of us believe that the spirit is an inner consciousness and therefore in dealing with it it seems appropriate to use colors, shapes, and forms that are not interpretations of the outer aspect of life.[3]

19

Craftsmanship

Jonson's art resolves itself into the pursuit and capture of the essence and rhythms of those moments of ecstatic visions of rare clarity (in themselves intangible and transient, however insistent) which arose not only from his conscious experience with the outer world but also from the depths of his subconscious. His sensations when confronting nature, particularly the landscape of the West and Southwest, made insistent demands for expression. Before they could escape he must fix them in his mind and make an effort to hold them within the substances of his craft. And those other feelings which arose spontaneously from within him also seemed to him to require perpetuation. Is it any wonder that before these transitory esthetic and spiritual presences could escape he must find the means for defining them? Is it any wonder that in the effort to achieve an art equivalent to his experience, he would suffer agonies of frustration over the problems and challenges of craftsmanship until he developed the technical mastery that gave him assurance?

The stresses of craftsmanship were constant in his formative years. Near the end of his first decade of work with the various media of drawing and painting, when he had already produced a substantial body of work, he lamented:

Oh what is one going to do? It seems that no matter what one does he is preparing his work for utter ruin. I'm beginning to wonder if it isn't best to throw all care to the winds and simply go ahead naturally. But then it isn't natural for me to be careless in that respect. Now with all my experimenting and reading I know no more than before. I have no safe way of proceeding. Each canvas is a new risk and I am doubtful concerning all the materials. So my problem for the next few years is to overcome these difficulties.[1]

Jonson's strength was in his enthusiasm, his inspiration, and his certainty of his mission. His uncertainties lay in the way he felt about the problems of craftsmanship and technique. No matter how competently and consummately he mastered his craft, his continuing anxiety was that it was not better. And when he had done his best, his worry was transferred to the future and the care of the work as a free object in the world.

The craftsman within the artist establishes him as a doer as well as a dreamer. However essential his vision, the artist's success or failure remains relative to his abilities as a craftsman. Thus the artist is concerned to perfect his skill because he knows that technical mastery is a requisite to the expression that reveals his inspiration. He is also concerned to complete, with assurance, a work that, because of his craftsmanship, will retain its fresh and original condition.

Another aspect of craftsmanship which is not necessarily evident in those two concerns is the care of the work after the artist has done his best at both the expressive and technical levels. If a work is to be enjoyed for its original values at a future time, every effort must be made to preserve those values. Jonson was well aware that mishandling and deterioration can diminish or destroy the qualities the artist has hoped to transmit. One of his objectives in founding the Jonson Gallery was to provide for his own works and those of other artists the protective care to which works of art are entitled.

When Jonson wrote, "[Art] is concerned with bringing about the fusion of matter with spirit, which is the object of creation itself,"[2] he was expressing one of the important if not major problems of craftsmanship to the solution of which he directed his attention.

Of the many generative ideas that modern art has inserted into the mainstream of the arts one of the most difficult to achieve, and yet most essential, is that of "the fusion of matter with spirit." How this is to be accomplished has occupied the minds of innumerable artists of this century, just as it has been a factor in primitive cultural art, in Asian art, and in religious art. The theories expounded by Kandinsky in *The Art of Spiritual Harmony* and Mondrian's concept of Neoplasticism had among their forerunners the poetry and prose of the Symbolist writers of the nineteenth century and the artists who came within the scope of the movement. It was as though the arts had arrived at one of those historical moments which presage a new era, which indeed was the case.

Under the impetus of the urge toward the spiritual in art, in the search for the means through which there could be "the fusion of matter with spirit," there developed almost as many ways as there have been artists making the search. There were those who through the lyrical gesture thought they had found something resulting from their passionate expressionistic art to which the term spiritual could be applied. At the other end of the spectrum were those artists of equally passionate persuasion who built systems of theory of varying degrees of complexity, who thought the applications of the theories would provide the desired end. Between these extremes there were numerous artists trying to solve the paradox in countless ways. It is not surprising, since the spiritual in art is reached by implication, that one solution of the problem is apt to be very different from another.

It is said that Kandinsky once expressed the notion that the day would come when artists would be able to communicate spiritual images without the use of paint and brushes. Such a thought would never occur to Jonson. To eliminate the materials and associated craftsmanship would be to eliminate the intent and purpose of their use, since it is through the transformation of materials that the spiritual is to be effected. Necessary to Jonson is the art object, a material, physical thing which in itself is the repository of the forces which transform matter. A perceptive witness of the art object can have sensuous responses to the material thing. He can also have the possibility of responding to the spirit implied by the kind of order impressed on the material by the creative act. Here was an extraordinary challenge that kept an artist of Jonson's persuasion hard at work: the challenge to eliminate the oppositon of inert matter by so transforming it as to evoke the immaterial creative force. He saw this activity as functional to all creativity and considered it a source of the spiritual in art.

20

The Airbrush

Jonson's painting procedures and modes of expression tended to evolve in an orderly progression which from painting to painting was imperceptible but which over a wider span showed great differences. Although sharp lines of cleavage between various periods are rare, there have been a number of events in his life as a painter which have had profound effects on his work, effects that sometimes seemed to appear with suddenness. Each of these events brought changes affecting his work over prolonged time spans.

We have already seen how his encounter with the Rocky Mountains of Colorado gave him a subject which exerted a powerful dominance and controlled his work for several years. Another of these events was his introduction to the New Mexican landscape near Santa Fe whereupon almost everything about his painting began to change as he submitted himself to the stimulating environment in which he found himself.

Of a different order was the adoption of the airbrush in 1938. This time it was not an aspect of nature that brought change but the possibilities the artist found in the uses of a painter's tool. The technical results were important in that they brought facility to the solution of a number of problems. If Jonson wanted to achieve a luminous quality of color through color spots, the controlled spatter effects of the airbrush eliminated the time-consuming business of spot-by-spot applications with brushes. There was for him, as for other artists, the worry in the use of oil paints that when the paint dried to its final condition, the result would not come up to expectation. But with the airbrush, using watercolor or tempera, there was immediate perception of the results as they would look ultimately.

Although the airbrush had been worked with at the Bauhaus, and Kandinsky and Moholy-Nagy had done serious work with it, Jonson struck upon its use independently.[1] His work with the airbrush elevated effects of the tool to a level on a par with the way touch is integrated in traditional brush painting. The peculiar grainy effect and the transparent shapes produced by the lightly spattered paint, consisting of tiny dots of color, were integrated into the formal organization of Jonson's work of this time. It became a property of his style. There is nothing else like his airbrush paintings in this period of American art, and they represent a unique contribution to painting because of the successful combination of a modern mechanical device and an extraordinarily inventive imagination.

The major benefit for Jonson was the sense of release, the new freedom which the airbrush provided. It brought the realization that the means was at hand for attaining the kind of expression to which he had long aspired. The execution of the work came closer to the flow of his feelings, and the use of the airbrush permitted his production to keep pace with the thronging ideas supplied by his imagination. In the simultaneous movement of ideas, feelings, and execution he found there was a direct relationship between that which called for expression and the process which concretized it. There was a sense of excitement as he contemplated the possibilities and the expanding horizon of his art. Little wonder, then, that it seemed to him that another frontier had been reached, and when he came to speak to the Chili Club about his spiritual experiences as an artist, he told about this, the fifth one:

> Santa Fe, 1938. In this year a wonderful and terrific experience occurred. Over a period of several months the whole method appeared in regard to creating simply and without strain in pure painting terms—the absolute. It was as if a complete cleansing process was in effect leveling off all the accumulation of subject matter, technique, experimentation and the agony accompanying them. . . .

In conclusion, Jonson said:

> I must make clear that these five aesthetic turning points stand as signposts along the way of many varieties of concepts and technical developments. They are the periods of great vision and

inspiration and not those many instances of emotional experiences that produce the particular work. They are the dominant or major supports for one's whole art.[2]

Jonson's viewpoint, his insistence on *quality,* and an obsessive need for release of his creative pressures to express compelling ideas and motifs made the facility of the airbrush an extraordinary asset. It seemed that for a time a mysterious affinity existed between the artist and the tool, for he accepted it unreservedly.

Throughout the airbrush works there is a constant high level of accomplishment. They speak Jonson's *design* and come as a fulfillment of the hope he had expressed in the early twenties that painting in "pure abstraction" was a possibility. It was a fortunate coincidence that he encountered and mastered the technique of the airbrush at precisely the time he had resolved the demands posed by landscape and the human figure.

Figure 43.   *Watercolor No. 18—1938.* 21x29 inches.

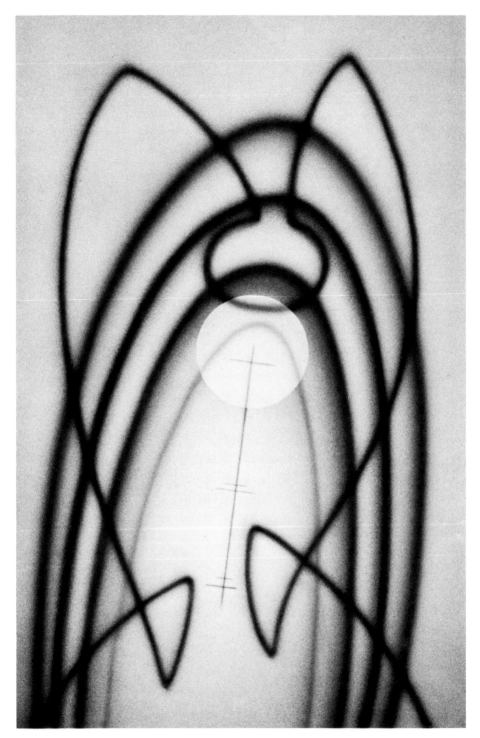

Figure 44. *Watercolor No. 17—1940.* 35x22 inches.

Figure 45. *Casein Tempera No. 6—1941.* 31x24 inches.

Carrying on the natural progressions of abstraction, he could develop works that were truly nonobjective and absolute. One can understand that Jonson could think of the release, both technical and emotional, afforded by this tool as a spiritual experience. The question whether Jonson would ever escape from the influence of his preoccupation with the landscape is answered in the affirmative. In these paintings the shapes, the rhythmic relationships, and the functioning of color in concord or dissonance as used in giving form to his ideas had to do with the relationship of part to part and how the parts, through their relationships, make up the whole.

In looking at such works, one sees the use of color, bright, mellow, and clear even in the darkest range; the interaction of delicate and vigorous rhythms; the range and multiplicity of shapes; and the astonishing transparencies. But it is in the feeling and emotion which these paintings arouse that one finds their meaning. The receptive viewer experiences a sensation which can be identified as spiritual, and one can feel the élan that brought this art into being. One can see that art is precisely the vehicle by which is expressed the otherwise inexpressible.

21

Color

Jonson's color is a world of its own. As a young painter he confessed that he was "lost in a puddle of paint," and exclaimed, "Color! I'm afraid I love it too much." This world of a "puddle of paint," this world of color which drew him in and so excited him when he entered it was one he would never leave. Throughout his life as a painter the lure of color and what it could do within a context drew him on. At whatever stage in the course of his development we find him, he is preoccupied with how to use color. If it was subject matter, color formed it; if it was motif, color shaped it; if it was idea, color gave it substance. His was a lifetime desire to release a purity of expression, and it was color that gave him the hope of liberating himself from the bondage imposed by matter. Paint itself is material, but its color, unlike the other ingredients that enter into a painting, can transcend itself and become alive, a magical property through which the artist can make matter expressive of the spiritual. When one seeks out those works that epitomize Jonson's strongest accomplishment, they are paintings in which his color functions in this way.

Jonson thought about color, talked about it, and theorized about it. Very early in his career he had a vision of and wanted to make a structurally expressive use of color, but he was unable to achieve it in the sense in which he used the phrase until well into the thirties.

When, on page 37, the reader was introduced to Jonson's 1917 painting *Light,* it was pointed out that the work amounted to a metaphor of light involving the use of the expressive energy of chromatics, though such use was subordinate to the symbolic import of his concept. This use of brilliant chromatics is rarely matched until after 1930 when color became strongly energized and reached its full importance in Jonson's paintings. His earlier works had employed color to establish mood and to reinforce the effects of light and shadow in the simulation of natural light. With his arrival in New Mexico he encountered an intense natural light which brought a vivid realization of what color could be and do. The intensification of color that developed under such light demanded a new vision of the possibilities, and a new spirit of freedom in Jonson's use of color had its beginnings.

The light of the high desert with its sharp contrasts of intense light and deep shade is often theatrical in effect.[1] Jonson brought this distinctive dramatic light to his semiabstract landscapes and, by recording it, he worked his way through its influence. Without losing his love for the southwestern light he was able to escape the appearance of natural light and develop toward a different kind of light arising solely through manipulations of color, dependent only on the needs of a specific painting.

Back in 1920 Jonson had discussed the subject in his diary:

> Color is not just pure color. It is much more. The tone or color throughout a picture should be very illusive in that it is a fine or close mixture. Large flat surfaces of color are apt to be lacking depth and mystery. . . . Color within a color, very closely related, properly applied using definite but subtle gradation, will give luminosity. This phenomenon holds true in greater or less degree with every form which receives light. By contrast of color and of value this luminosity can be accentuated. Using this principle of definite color spots I believe it is possible, by proper relation and gradation, to obtain this luminosity in any value, tone, or color. Even gray will take its place in this list.

> The thing is to have the color spots closely enough related so that they are not obvious and do not vibrate among themselves. I have come to the conclusion that the space or mass should vibrate but not the color spots within the mass. By vibrate in the first, I mean the mass should be alive and have luminosity. In the second or color spots, I mean the spots themselves as complimentaries move and therefore show as separate color spots.

All this concerning luminosity is the biggest step I have discovered and taken. It seems to me it is a natural outgrowth from juxtaposition of color.[2]

There was a long-term development of the idea until the process came into full and independent use. The remark about "a fine or close mixture" is a good description of the color effects possible with the airbrush which, as we have seen, he adopted eighteen years later. The fact that, aside from its other contributions to his work, the airbrush could readily provide a means for obtaining luminosity explains in part the enthusiasm with which Jonson related to this tool and welcomed it into his technical equipment.

What he sought had two major values. One had to do with personal use of color as a lyrical or dramatic theme. The other had to do with what he called quality in pigmentation. When Jonson refers to *quality* in a painting, it is often this particularized type of quality of which he is thinking. It has been one of the crucial factors in his expectations of and decisions concerning what is good in his own painting and that of others. In a talk given in 1949 he explained his viewpoint:

The type of quality I refer to is that of the material used to project the concept. It is a state or condition of the material such as oil, watercolor and tempera paint. It has to do with a kind of optical-tactile feel, that is it is as if one can feel it through the eyes. It has something to do with richness and rightness. It possesses a mystery and by some phenomenon it appears to come to life. It is the result of taking the natural quality of the pigment as it comes from the tube and improving on it to the extent that it becomes significant in its relationships with other colors and of a truer value as well as richness, whether glossy or matte in finish. In establishing quality in the pigmentation a certain amount of manipulation occurs. As a result texture develops. Therefore, in seeing the quality one also sees the texture and these two are inseparable. Usually, the finer the quality the better the texture. Most color pigments of like binder appear almost identical in quality and texture as they come from the tubes. But each good painter transforms them in his way and his way is usually different from all others. Therefore I imagine there are thousands of different qualities with their attendant textures. To detect this results in a deeper comprehension of the particular painting. This item of quality in pigmentation is one of the wonderful things in painting whether in works hundreds of years old or contemporary.

Quality has nothing to do with the type of painting for it can be realistic, surrealistic, impressionistic, abstract or absolute. In all types it is possible to have paint quality or the lack of it. All our great artists are superb in pigment quality for that is one of the things that make them great.

A work lacking in quality cannot approach the spiritual. But the work that surpasses or transcends the natural and undeveloped aspect of the paint can approach and at times move directly into the spiritual providing the feeling and attitude on the part of the painter deal with the inner spirit of man rather than the outer and physical.[3]

However, the type of quality of which he spoke was not the whole meaning of *quality* in the distinctive sense Jonson intended by the word. It had far-reaching implications, for *quality* in this sense entered into and affected all the elements that his *design* idea comprised. Concerning this extended and, in some respects, almost unique conception of quality, he wrote:

It seems to me that when a painter has accomplished quality through purity of inner vision, fulfillment and pleasure can result both on the part of the painter and the audience. By quality I mean that elusive and mysterious sort of film that binds the work together through integration of the color or tone with the shape or form, the line with the rhythm, etc., these in accord with the texture so that the work has a tactile kind of richness. In the finest realization there can result a discernment of special illumination or luminosity.

Purity of inner vision indicates a sense of heightened order, resulting from the impact of an emotional or mental comprehension, or both, visualized from the inner self and not from the surface aspect of the world.

To the word "pleasure" I attach a special meaning—namely, that because of the experience of quality a sensation beyond the ordinary can take us into the realm of new emotions and we can thereby reach a level of ecstasy on which we are able to rise above the purely physical into the field of the spiritual.[4]

Thus it is seen that, although quality in pigmentation was in Jonson's view a requisite to good painting, there were far broader implications to his use of the term *quality*. It became for him "that elusive and mysterious sort of film," invisible as an entity, but which nevertheless is there in a good painting, one so organized as to produce its presence, a real necessity for the fulfillment of his ideals concerning what good painting must be.

In the foregoing discussion of quality in pigmentation Jonson pointed out that "in seeing quality one also sees texture and these two are inseparable." The inseparability of quality and texture has caused Jonson to make texture an important expressive value in his work, one which should command our conscious attention.

The expressive possibilities of texture are presented to us in innumerable ways. As an introduction to seeing texture as a feature of Jonson's work a few general types, by no means exhaustive, may serve to draw attention to this item which, under close scrutiny, can prove to be most rewarding.

One aspect of texture for which Jonson has found frequent use, particularly in his oils, has been the optical alteration of color by the physical shaping of the paint. The body of the paint is so manipulated that it intrudes into actual space, coming forward to meet the eye while picking up light which in turn modifies the color it envelops. The union of the color with this kind of texture produces a color quality distinctive to these works.

Another family of textures may be found in works done with brushes or other tools, which in their use give the applications of paint unique, imaginative characteristics. Depending on the materials of which they are made, their shapes, and their sizes, brushes can give their own peculiar marks. Depending on how these individual characteristics are controlled, brushes can set up activities within the paint which result in a variety of responses such as forming, or being a part of, the main rhythms and movements of the painting. Allowed to declare themselves, the marks of the artist's tools can establish an identity of their own and become an intrinsic element in the work of art. They add another dimension to a work that might lack certain operative dynamics had the tool been used in such a way as to neutralize the effect of its identity. For instance, Jonson's paintings done with the brayer (Figure 52 is an example) include textures that could be obtained with no other tool. Often these textures are very intricate, beautiful, and fascinating in their variety and unique nature. Although they might be considered almost ends in themselves, the textures actually contribute to the establishment of shapes and rhythms while enhancing the paint to an extraordinary liveliness.

Utterly unlike the previously mentioned textures are those in paintings whose textures are derived neither from the physical manipulation of the paint nor from exploiting the individual characteristics of brushes or other tools. Particularly in works done in spray and spatter techniques, the texture becomes almost an illusionary one, and the paint itself seems bodiless since the actual paint layer, no matter how many shapes underlie or overlie one another, is extremely thin. The varied sizes of spots of color and the mixture of colors possible to this method seem often to dissolve the solidity of the picture plane as such, and there is a floating backward and forward in a colorful, light-permeated space. At close range there usually is a grainy sort of texture made up of innumerable granules of color which, when the work is viewed at greater distance, blend into a luminescent smoothness.

In these and each of the many other ways Jonson handles his paint to form textures, there develops a transformation of the paint and its color through which we find a separate source of pleasure. In its ultimate use, and as its primary purpose, within the context of the total unity of the work, texture intensifies the sensation of rich, fresh color.

In the mid thirties, Jonson began a series which, at the time, he termed Configuration. He developed the series to utilize an experience he was having with a certain type of color relationship. He had observed that when two colors very close in value are juxtaposed there is not only the vibration he associated with *luminosity* but another, different kind of vibration. Forthwith, he set out to use it in the new series.

In these I have thought of a kind of dissonance in color playing a part in the composition. [A] music term I know but there is not a word in painting that would state the item. To a considerable extent I have failed in this particular respect in that color insists upon going harmonious. Now what I am after is exactly the same thing in music except that here it will be color. In other words a complete rhythm built like a discord which becomes resolved and will add a further kick, as it were, to the sensation of color movement.[5]

A few months after he had so written to his brother Arthur, he changed the title of the series from Configuration to *Chromatic Contrasts* (Figures 46, 47, and 62, and Plate 5). He wrote, "That is just what they are. One important element in them is to establish a kind of dissonance in color. It is this dissonance item that distinguishes them from the *Figuration* series."[6] This new item became the third member of a color triad: tonal—brilliant—dissonant. Dissonance can be simple, subtle, or a complexity of such juxtapositions. It can be an incidental factor in a work, or it can be the central motif.

Several years later he expressed to the author his interest in dissonance in this way:

It is quite possible that the whole of the *Chromatic Contrast* group falls into a type of the dynamic for the simple reason that within the use of color this way it cuts across the established idea of consonant harmony. If it is possible to incorporate with this [new] type of harmony, shape and line which is either in harmony with that perhaps disharmony, or in disharmony with disharmony, we may find ourselves on a very, very interesting path.[7]

It was an interesting path because, resulting from his interest in the vibration he called dissonance, has come the longest and most persistent series of Jonson's paintings. The first of the *Chromatic Contrasts* was painted in 1935 and there have been thirty-four of them, the most recent dated 1965. The long span in the production of the series and the fact that there are such paintings done in oils, watercolors, and acrylics indicate with what insistence the concept has occupied Jonson's interest.

The *Chromatic Contrasts* involve other elements of form and rhythm, for rarely does a single item become so dominant in this artist's interest as to override everything else. In his desire to realize *design* fully and to make

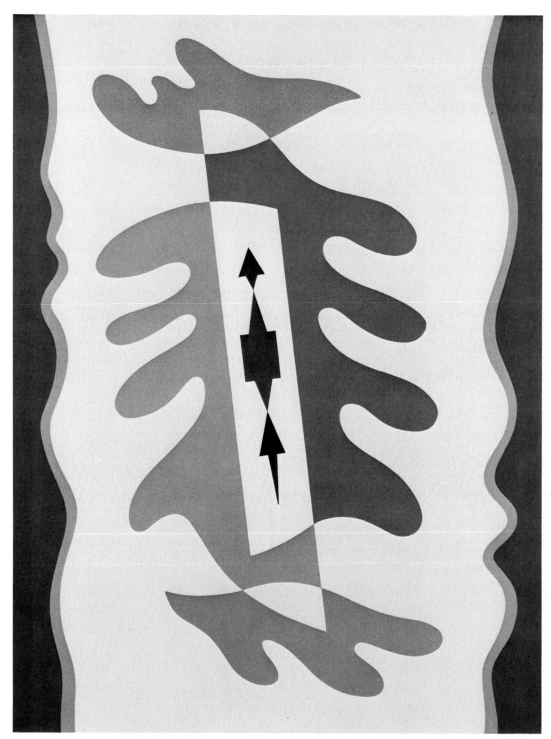

Figure 46.   *Chromatic Contrasts No. 14 (Oil No. 8—1943)*. 40x32 inches.

Figure 47. *Chromatic Contrasts No. 30*
(*Polymer No. 11—1958*). 22½x40 inches.

Figure 48. *Pictographical Composition No. 7*
(*Oil No. 17—1946*). 28x36 inches.

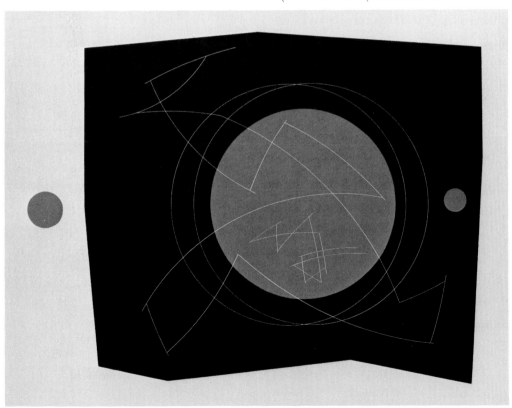

quality a prime requisite, any single factor such as dissonance, however preponderant in a specific painting, was meshed into other constituents in such a way as to make the work itself a type of harmony consistent with his esthetic requirements.

The most recent group of paintings listed as belonging to a series is the *Pictographical Compositions* (Figure 48), seventeen in number, done in 1946 and 1947. Despite the implications of the general title, they do not make use of the motifs or shapes of Indian rock wall painting or carving. These works illustrate how an influence can stimulate and be made use of in ways which, though a relationship is not entirely absent, are quite independent of the presumed influence. Of these works, Jonson wrote:

> They present little if any clue as to what they are based on. The title is the only clue and it may be misleading for it could be taken to mean a particular pictograph or petroglyph which is not the case. It is simply an emotional organization established in *design* terms upon thinking of pictographs and petroglyphs in general. The physical connection is the use of the incised line and the admixture of sand with the paint in certain shapes.[8]

In the course of this study of Jonson's work a great deal of attention has been given to the works done in a series. One might suppose, therefore, that most of his work was so done. However, these groups have been used as an expedient way of tracing the various directions in his work, since the paintings they comprise characterize what was being done in general at the time they were painted. Actually, the works of the series represent only a modest part of Jonson's production. Year after year single painting after painting came out of a general attitude based on a diversity of stimulations, painting problems, and his creative drive. Works occurred because they had to. This necessity to paint could easily have resulted in mediocre works. Because of Jonson's serious formulation of his goals and his persistent demand that his work should be technically right, of sound craftsmanship, the overall quality is remarkably even. They serve to illustrate the kind of beauty he hoped to achieve. It is as though a plateau had been reached, for in these paintings Jonson had found a complete harmony between himself and his means of expression.

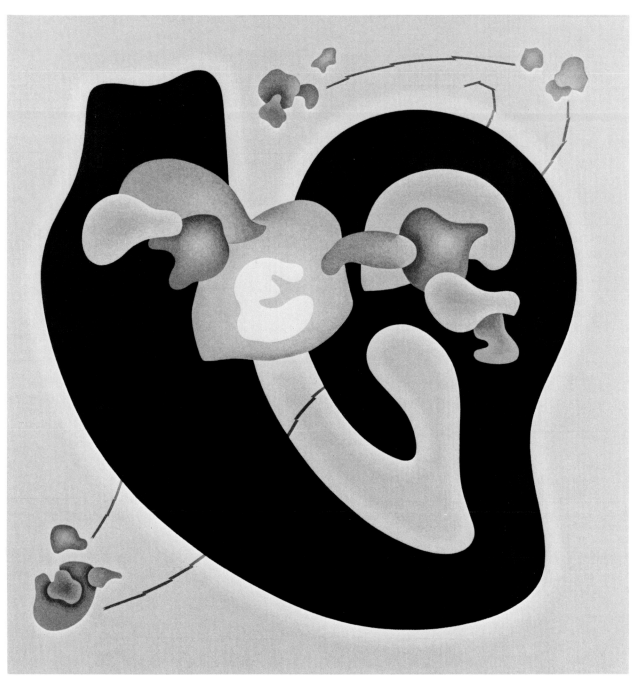

Figure 49. *Oil No. 10–1941.* 40x40 inches.

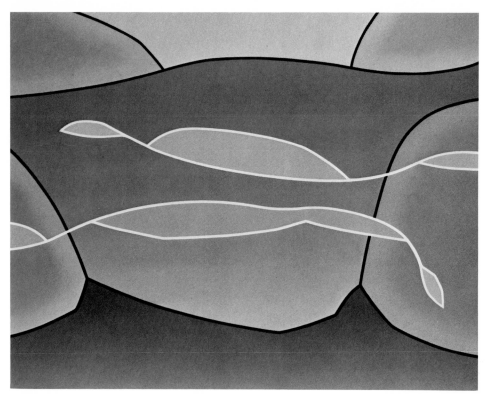

Figure 50.   *Oil No. 6—1952.* 38x48 inches.

Figure 51.   *Oil No. 7—1957.* 50x60 inches.

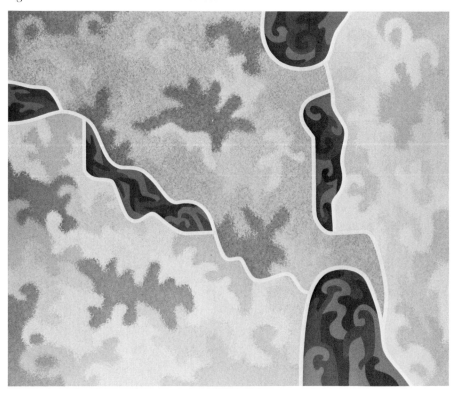

22

Toward Fulfillment

In studying the development of Jonson's work, and taking into account his writings, his talk, and the paintings themselves, indications can be found that he has been reaching for and stressing something more than the capabilities ordinarily derived from the simple elements of painting. In interpreting this direction we can find that his art is in a transcendent realm where the imagination creates by illusion through the material, the feelings, visions, and meanings of the painter's experience. The artist shows through his art that by subtle means he can transform things to create the illusion of yet other things in order to present to the viewer his experience.

All the constituents that have gone into the accomplishment of the final effect of the work have been grouped into various combinations and have become so meshed, woven, and formed into bundles of effects that, by their resolution within the total work, they reach beyond the immediate senses, straight to the emotions. Although such effects may be, within themselves, beyond specific logical definition, it is their quality of plasticity, their sensitivity to nuances of meaning, that make them ideal instruments for the resolution of felt ideas. Advanced by the creative mind, within the context of his work, we are made aware that something is stirring us even if we are not conscious of what it is that moves us. Used creatively, they have emerged within each work as a definite effect, clear and reasonable, and have been produced to meet the value criteria set up by the painter.

We have seen how Jonson, in discovering and developing the components that would serve him in working through to a full expression of his art, had posited *quality* and *luminosity*. *Simplicity,* which was also imperative to him, was integrated into his style through the long processes of abstraction. Added to these were other components, among them *rhythm* and *gesture,* to fill out the complex which he termed *design.*

By *rhythm,* Jonson means the flow of order through a painting. The work of art presents itself to him as a sensation of rhythmic order. *Rhythm* results from relationships. Flow and movement depend on the various ways in which relationships are established through the use of space, shapes, colors, lines, edges, and contrasts. Since flow and movement are not actual but are created in our perception, we pick them up by following lines and edges, by shifting from plane to plane, by following color sequences and divisions of the area, and by skipping from contrast to contrast. As we develop empathy with what we are seeing, the feeling of flow and movement is created, and *rhythm* is established. *Rhythm* is ordered variations such as intervals, spacing, recurrence, and regularities, but it is also built of opposing forces whose interplay can alternate tension and release. Hence there is a dynamic contribution to the overall aliveness of the work and a contribution to the integration of the unity of the work in its entirety.

For many years, Jonson's procedures included drawings of his ideas. In some cases these drawings were worked out in detail, so that the projected painting would come as close as he could contrive to his intentions. Even so, the carefully planned painting would sometimes, in the course of production, develop a new focus and become so changed that the final version differed from the drawing which preceded it. Jonson accepted these happenings as a natural part of creativity; the conception had expanded, or a technical discovery was made that recommended a change of direction or a difference in intensification. As a result, in more recent years the preliminary drawings for paintings have tended to become mere skeletons of the designs which the conceived works are intended to realize. When he began developing the improvisational approach, the usual procedures were gradually departed from and the painting eventually came as a single *gesture.*

There came a recognition that in a high moment of creation there was an emotional response to what the eye was seeing and what was being felt through the generative force. There was a recognition that something was occurring that had the burn of truth to it, a cosmic rightness. Its projection became the source of the painter's action. To seize that moment would be to release his concept in a powerful *gesture* that would fix on the canvas a form equivalent to the force of his emotion. *Gesture* thus represents a state of being, as well as of acting, which at the peak and instant of reaching its full force combines all the elements together to make a painting.

In doing improvisational works, Jonson learned that all the factors that had been incorporated in his *design* had become so deeply imbedded in his subconscious as well as his conscious mind that he observed them almost automatically in the act of painting. The execution of the work came closer to the flow of his feelings. In the simultaneous movement of ideas, feelings, and execution he discovered that there was a direct relationship between the feelings, which called for expression, and the process which concretized them. The paintings that resulted embodied the mental impression and the physical action as a single *gesture* that reinforced the expression of the one and the freedom of the other, so that they became a unit.

Gesture is related to, and in part grew out of, Jonson's concern with *rhythm*. One of the functions of *gesture* in the concept of *design* is to bring to the flow and movement of the work the feeling of immediacy. Because in a physical sense *gesture* involves action, it requires the manipulation of the paint within a limited time span. It becomes the function of the immediate moment, and consequently it eliminates nonsustaining detail and stresses the primary aspects of a single idea while also stressing continuity and movement. Thus it is seen that *gesture* is related not only to *rhythm* but is also intimately related to *simplicity*.

However carefully and deliberately the artist may perform the preliminary work leading toward the finished painting, the act itself through *gesture* unifies the mental and physical constituents of a work. *Gesture*, as this artist uses it, is no mere physical movement in a measured space. It is an extraordinary focus on the time of execution when thought, wish, and inspiration are fused with the spontaneity of the act. It becomes a dynamic expression of coordination, a coordination of all the parts that produce a unity formed by passion. Achieved by intention, it arrests inspirational energy within the work with an intensity of concentration that animates the entire painting. It contains a sweeping movement of intent that breathes spirit into the body of the work of art, and in so doing it consummates the

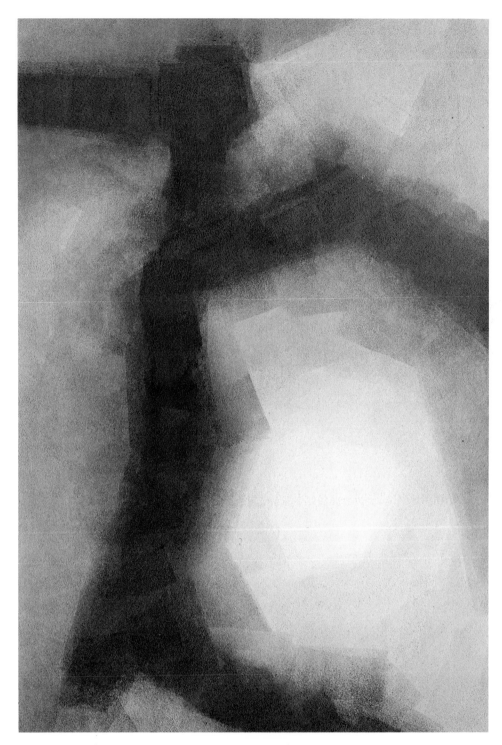

Figure 52. *Oil No. 6—1956 (Improvisation)*. 37x25 inches.

purpose of the *unifying principle* to give it the stamp of style and conviction.

After having established the reliability of improvisation or its equivalent through the use of the airbrush and conventional brushes in watercolors and tempera, Jonson went on to a different method, that of oils done with a brayer. The overall movement of the brayer used spontaneously with great freedom, the resulting textures, and a simple color scheme produced distinctive and fascinating paintings which involved the very essence of *gesture.*

During the fifties he produced a group of oil paintings that are in fact, if not always in title, improvisations. In them there is a free and impulsive maneuvering over the area. The impulse is what is seen optically at the time of creation, thus contrasting with earlier oils which had been visualized mentally and usually carefully charted. Under the hand of the artist the painting grows on the surface. The tool is allowed to declare itself in textures otherwise impossible to achieve, and the textured color becomes a predominant effect in the completed work. In some of the brayer works and also in some oils painted with brushes there is a further element of improvisation through the use of various other instruments to achieve straight lines, curves, and circles which set up counter rhythms and contrasts to color and texture.

Concerning the works we have called improvisations, Jonson wrote:

> The intention in the improvisations is to bombard the eye by a spontaneity of direct execution either in a calm or an active environment as the case may be. My hope is that, because of the long and constant striving for control with all the elements of painting, it is possible to invent, create, and improvise not only in a spirit of abandonment, but with a physical attack as well, in causing the surface to come to life. If the work is alive, I believe it must possess the ingredients that make it a dynamic and pregnant statement.[1]

23

The Artist's Materials

A painting is itself a material thing which is influenced by the substances with which it is made. The respect for and development of the qualities of the materials used in painting are necessary to the effectiveness of the work of art for they contain in themselves potentials for beauty, pleasure, and sensuous rewards. The various qualities of materials exist for better or worse. It is the task of the artist to realize their highest potentials and enhance them into expressiveness.

The artist's love for the materials of his craft is as old as art itself. The material which he molds, the tools he uses, the way he employs his hands and mind—all these together wed the artist to his instruments. There arises a type of empathy between the artist and his materials in which the paints, the tools, and the way he uses them become an expression of the man as well as the means.

Excellence, refinement, and certainty of skills are reflected in the use of materials. The sense of harmony between the artist and his means, the certainty and assurance with which he handles them, attest his mastery. Whatever the artist wishes to say must be said through the many possibilities contained in materials. Their eloquence must support his eloquence.

The evocation of eloquence from raw substances, persuading the ingredients and elements of his art to reveal themselves in expression, became for Jonson part of the mainstream of his endeavor. The constant effort to transform matter into sensation brought with it a sensitivity to discovery, for the conversion of matter to sensation was not only to be found by imposing spirit upon matter but by releasing out of matter its inherent spirit.

One of the results of Jonson's use of the airbrush with watercolor and tempera was, as it were, a new look at the media as the media themselves attained a new look. At times in these works it is almost as though a different, unrecognized medium had been used, thus demonstrating the ability of the material to respond to the artist's demands and to expand into previously unsuspected potentials. Similarly, in the oils done with the brayer, while the medium remains indubitably itself, it seems to have undergone a change as though something had happened to transform it. Here the artist and the tool, working together with the paint, seem to have opened a new area in what had seemed to be fully explored territory.

In a related technique, though quite unlike the brayer look, are the paintings in which poured oils are so manipulated as to result in forms that are freely developed in the wet and liquid paint. This, however, was a technique which was more fully exploited when the medium was acrylic polymer (Figure 53).

The pleasure of materials and their potentials became more acute in Jonson's work. More and more the eloquence of materials became the theme of his paintings. There is a lively sense of wonder derived from the manipulation of materials revealed in textured colors which cause the painting to move and vibrate with their energies. These works are impressive in that their technical characteristics remain pure. They are free and yet they remain ordered. A sensitivity to means is highly dramatized and the method itself becomes part of the paintings' "subject matter."

Nor were such trends limited to paintings. The black and white of a group of seventeen spontaneous nonobjective drawings done in 1957 likewise fall within the same attitude and fulfill the same criteria (Figure 54).

In 1957 a fully coordinated, stabilized, and complete line of acrylic polymer paints became available to artists. Their versatility, flexibility, rapid drying, and permanence soon gained Jonson's enthusiastic acceptance. Once again, as had been the case with the air brush and the brayer, a technical factor served as a source of confidence, release, and inspiration. Watercolor and tempera were dropped immediately, and no oils were painted after 1960. Other than three lithographs in 1965, Jonson's entire subsequent production has been in acrylics.[1]

Jonson naturally wondered of what this new medium was capable and set about exploring its possibilities. He used sable and bristle brushes in a

Figure 53.   *Oil No. 3—1959.* 20x28 inches.

Figure 54.   *Drawing No. 6—1957.* Ink, 19x27 inches.

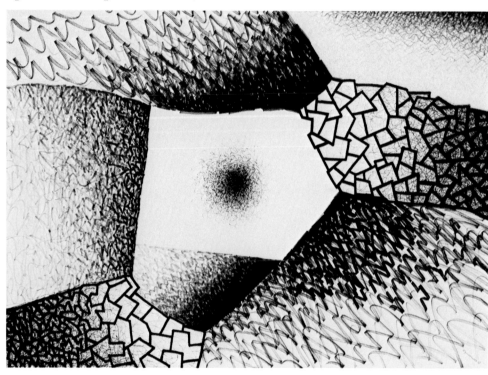

variety of techniques including an intricate system of hatching that produced beautiful and intriguing effects. He tried pouring the acrylic polymer onto his panel and stirring it into fantastic, frequently elaborate labyrinths of color and design. In other works he used a roller for exact, even layers of paint. Happily, he found a sprayer without a needle which allowed him in sprayed works a wide range of spots of color from very fine to comparatively large.

Aggregates, such as sand, sawdust, wood shavings, and powdered Plexiglas, immersed in the acrylic paint brought fresh effects to textures. He worked out a system of pouring paint onto glass to dry and then retrieving the shape thus discovered or invented for attachment to his painting. Into these shapes he sometimes stirred miscellaneous colors to produce intricate patterns related to, but always different from, the earlier stirred acrylics. Such pieces of paint could be cut and trimmed to provide any shape desired for a given work.

Some paintings contain brushwork, spraying, and attached pieces. Others are done entirely by spraying, and some contain no spraying whatever. A few works consist of a single large piece of the paint material prepared on glass and attached to a panel.

If ever an artist found his true medium, Jonson did when he turned to the acrylic polymers. In them he found an affinity that canceled out all previous affinities. Completely free from technical worries and in full control of the medium, he could invent shapes in seemingly inexhaustible variety, be as elaborate or as austere as he wished, revel in color from the mildest tonality to a crashing brilliance.

The significant direction and final effects of Jonson's acrylic paintings is away from the intimate and introspective look of many of the earlier works. In contrast, due to a shift in the scale and a new attitude toward the use of his materials, they have a monumental look. There is in them a movement from tightly knit organizations, even in the improvisations, to a broader, open statement. Compared to many of the earlier works the *Polymers* use color boldly, aggressively, in direct physical vibrancy. The best of the acrylic paintings stand at the apogee of Jonson's maturity.

In 1973 Jonson began a series of works that emphasized and extended his interest in the subject of space in painting, a subject that has been one of his major interests throughout the years.

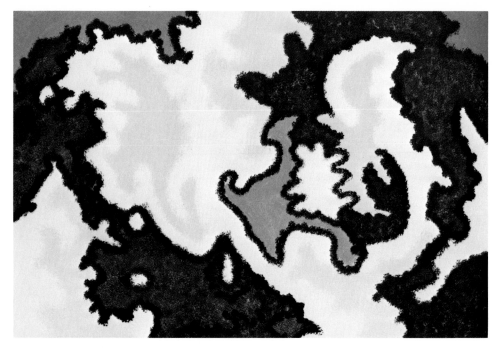

Figure 55. *Polymer No. 1—1957.*
Acrylic, 24x36 inches. Sable and bristle brushes.

Figure 56. *Polymer No. 5—1957.*
Acrylic, 48x54 inches. Sable brush.

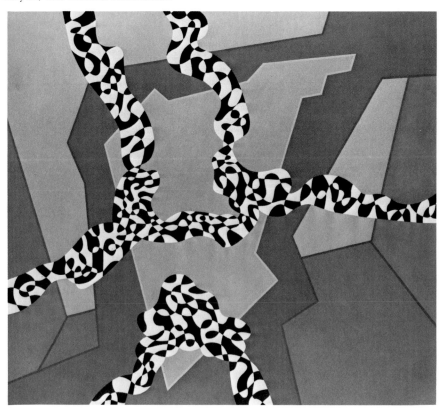

Figure 57. *Polymer No. 29—1959*. Acrylic, 57x45 inches. Bristle brush.

Figure 58. *Polymer No. 16—1959*. Acrylic, 30x24 inches. Poured paint.

Figure 59. *Polymer No. 39—1970.* Acrylic, 48x39 inches. Fine spray.

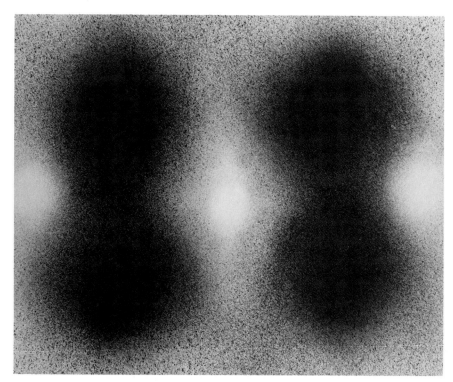

Figure 60. *Polymer No. 10—1971.*
Acrylic, 39x48 inches. Coarse spray.

Figure 61. *Polymer No. 33—1964.*
Acrylic, 45x54 inches. Aggregates included.

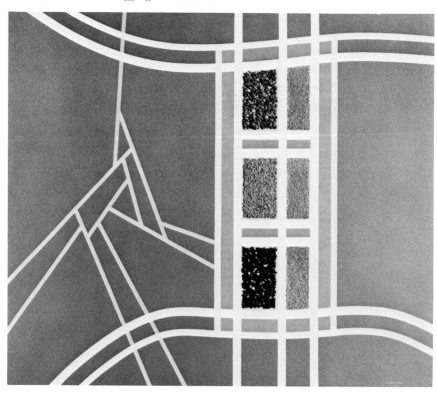

Figure 62. *Chromatic Contrasts No. 32 (Polymer No. 1—1965).*
Acrylic, 48x39 inches. Brush, spray, attached pieces.

In painting, space is one of the important illusions that arrest, captivate, and intrigue the viewer. It is to the word "illusion" that we must turn in explaining space as a part of the formative subject matter of Jonson's work.

Perceptions of space in painting are illusionary. Our perceptual equipment reads experience in terms of the three dimensions. Even the much-valued two-dimensional surface of the picture plane as it is stressed in modern art is an illusion. The two-dimensional surface of the picture plane provides stable points in space to act as fulcrums for the inward and outward formation of effects of space. This is done in countless ways. In combination and contrast these effects can produce remarkable results.

In establishing space the artist can place the viewer in almost any position in space: looking downward, from a distance, or from any other position at the artist's wish.

In Jonson's paintings space can undulate in rhythm with the movement of line. Through color there can be recession and advancement. Through transparency space can lie simultaneously at an indefinite number of levels. Through drawing there can be an overlapping of areas and penetrations by perspectives which may move in different directions. Through tonal gradations there can be a recession of space into atmosphere. Through texture, space can advance from the surface of the painting to touch the eyes. These many qualities of space are among the basic reasons for Jonson's love of absolute painting, for in this kind of painting spatial experience of a wide variety can be had.

With the series of works begun in 1973 Jonson has presented us with yet another aspect of space and has produced a group of interesting works in which one or more open shapes are cut through the primary picture plane, which is usually made of some type of hardboard. In others, solid two-dimensional shapes are so inserted into the area within a frame as to leave openings through which, in both cases, the nature of the wall is revealed and incorporated into the effect of the painting. The spatial illusion created by these works is unlike that elaborated in any of Jonson's previous investigations of space. It is an actual visual introduction of the character of the wall itself with the space between the wall and the face of the painting brought into an esthetic relationship with the picture plane. In some of these works there are several planes set at different levels. The illusionary

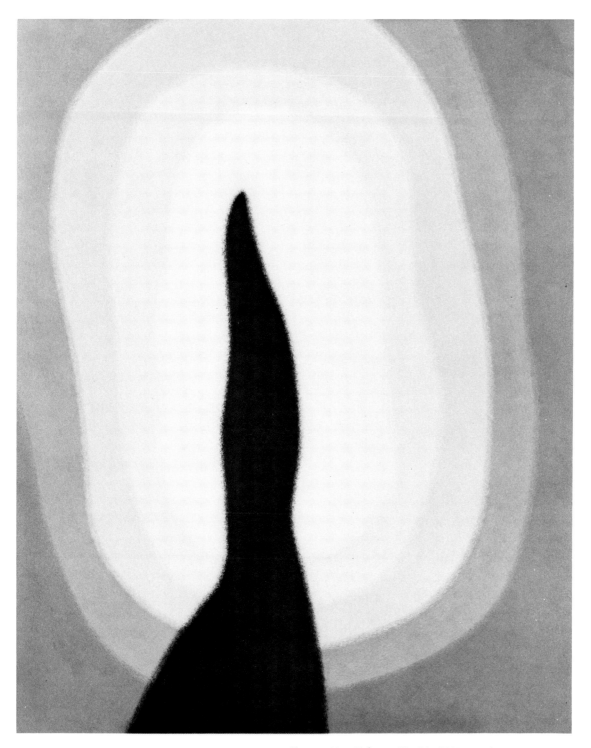

Figure 63. *Polymer No. 21—1961*. Acrylic, 45x36 inches.

Figure 64. *Polymer No. 32—1964.* Acrylic, 48x72 inches.

Figure 65. *Polymer No. 28—1965*. Acrylic, 75½x37 inches.

Figure 66. *Polymer No. 28—1966*. Acrylic, 31x27 inches.

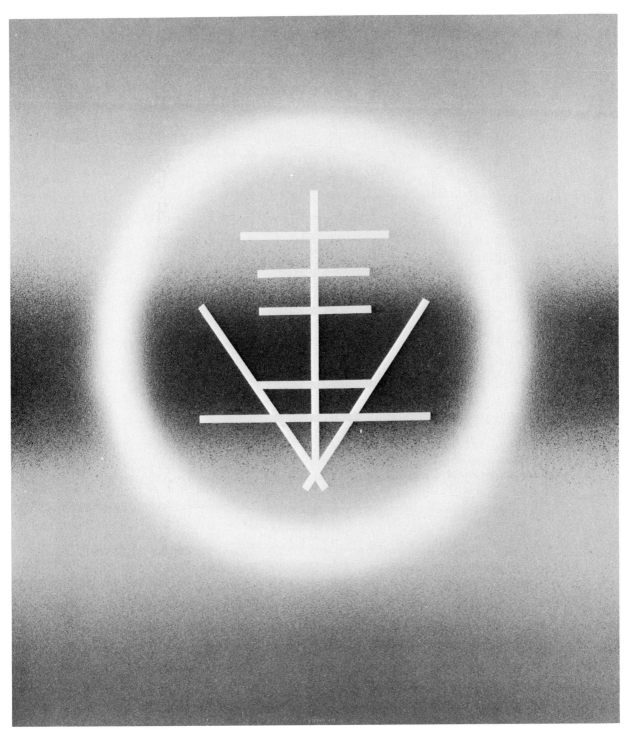

Figure 67. *Polymer No. 31—1970.* Acrylic, 30x27 inches.

Figure 68. *Polymer No. 18—1973.* Acrylic, 48x33 inches.

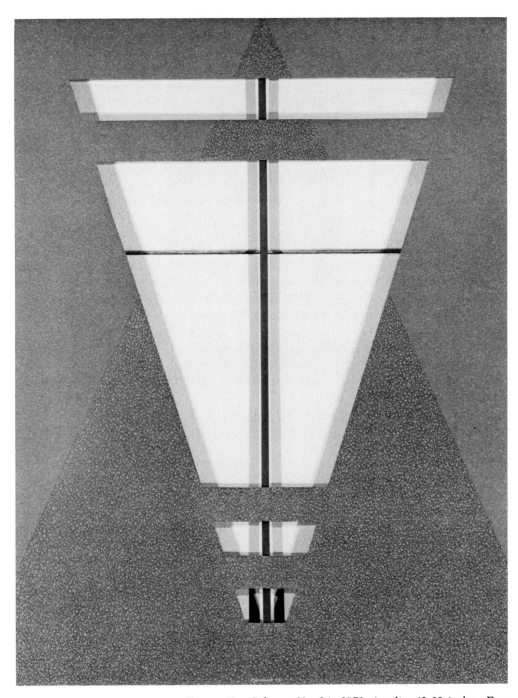

Figure 69. *Polymer No. 24—1973.* Acrylic, 42x33 inches. Four cutout open spatial shapes. The white areas and the adjoining intermediate values, which are cast shadows, show the wall on which the painting is hung. The line that crosses the large opening is the hanging groove which thus becomes a part of the work. Compare with Plate 8.

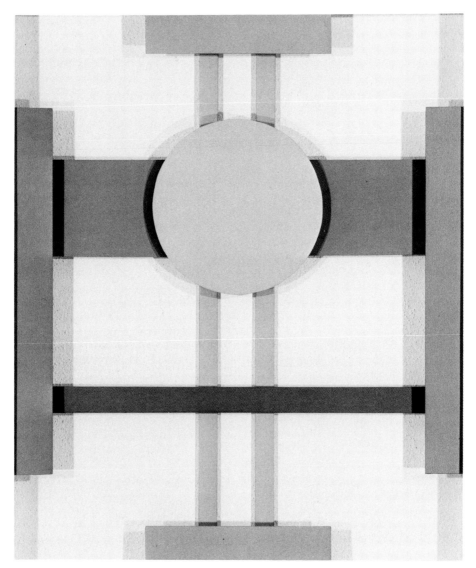

Figure 70. *Polymer No. 7—1974.* Acrylic, 29x24½ inches.
Various shapes set into an open frame.

effect, when caught, is of each plane moving forward toward the front rather than receding from it as ordinary visual logic would have us expect. Jonson draws the "reality" of living space into his esthetic space by tying the two together so that the content of the painting, which in some respects might be termed a construction, and the environment in which it is seen form a harmonious relationship. Instead of the usual contrast between the painting and its surroundings, the result is the cooperation of the one with the other.

24

Culmination

Of the several main ideas that have dominated Jonson's life the foremost has been to work out his salvation[1] within the terms of painting. He wanted his work to become a symbol of unity and order that would express what he had made of his life both in body and spirit. He has been devoted to life through the art of painting, not painting for its own sake but as a way of life, as an expression of what intelligent and sensitive living can apprehend and communicate.

Jonson has said, "I feel that I wish to include all with no special emphasis on any. That is one reason why I have no formal religion, no theory of philosophy, no social status, no political membership, no esoteric convictions. To paint is enough for if that painting is great enough it must include and at the same time surmount all these."[2]

Surely he must have been confronted with many questions, questions that could be answered only by the living and working processes themselves. How was one to develop within one's chosen discipline, with its inherent limitations, and yet retain and even heighten human values? Could he, as an artist, satisfactorily integrate himself with life as a whole person and at the same time so develop as an artist that he would merge with and extend the mainstream of art? At the heart of any questioning was the crucial one of whether he could produce works that would express his experience and his character in terms of style.

It took great personal effort to resolve such questions. It made the creative issue often a desperate one. As he wrote, "It is quite a problem: how at the same time create and live that beauty. That is the question."[3]

The urgency Jonson felt about his creative work arose because he always seemed to feel himself to be on the threshold of a vision beyond his current experience with the promise of a breakthrough to another dimension of qualitative values. He sought to express qualities that grew out of his experience as a human being, as a sensitive investigative intelligence, and as a painter involved with plastic problems. The resolution of these factors in esthetic terms was the crux of the challenge.

The development of Jonson's creative processes and his art have shown a constant progression toward purity. In the pursuit of the purification of his art in the act of creation he also purified himself. In achieving a creative release he purged himself of unwanted content no longer necessary to his growth. In liberation he arrived at a condition which progressively resulted in a clearer image of himself and his role as an artist. Therefore he could function more certainly in the expression of what he was and show what a totally free and creative person could do under conditions he had established as best for himself and the free expression of his esthetic choices and human values. In the search for the unity, order, and rhythm that could give form to the formless and the spiritual to the material, he traversed the route which led to his concept of the *unifying principle,* the *design,* which became the vitalizing influence on his art.

Jonson saw *design* not only as a painter's approach but also as a discipline within which the whole person could function. He believed that in approaching the creative act the whole person can function in a normal and healthy way with a free flow of his emotional energies and with the painting growing out of the painting context. It follows that a work of art will result that is consonant to the person and to the art of painting.

He found that the unity and order that he desired in his art were to be obtained through formal principles. If he wished to express himself in terms of unity and order, then it was necessary to seek out absolute means of control. Without such control, factors unamenable to it could exert themselves to distort the art through which he sought expression. Control therefore became a necessity for constructive effort and was requisite for the affirmation of the idealism invested in his concepts of order and unity.

In the beginning he described the direction his art would take as his "straight as a die road."[4] Consequently, he worked toward specific ends. One was "to realize that which exists as pure expression." Another was "something like creating a new rhythm, a new reality." These two ideas were fundamental to his concept of *design,* and through many years of effort the goals which were first clearly visualized in 1922 had by the thirties reached a degree of achievement that, as the years progressed, fulfilled and culminated his earlier hopes.

One of the objectives in the earlier stages of *design* was to adapt it to the objective world around him as evidenced in the landscapes of the twenties. A second was to show in variation the creative possibilities an artist may discover in the shapes found in homogeneous groups such as the digits and the alphabet. A third was to set up a group of created relationships that functioned in his painting as an environment expressing the unity and order which are the essence of his concept and are best realized in the nonrepresentational works.

The concept of *design* as a working thesis and living attitude provided a flexible and expanding tool to formulate Jonson's creative statements. In his painting its function was to establish order and unity, to supply shapes and their relationships, to determine the character of the organization whereby such components as *luminosity* and *rhythm* in accord with *simplicity* and *gesture*, with the whole conditioned by *quality*, would perform to their utmost. Once we realize that Jonson has increasingly derived his inspiration from these synthesized components, made them his major agents, and given them meaning within the overall concept of *design*, we may realize the measure of his achievements.

To appreciate Jonson's *design* we must see and feel parts built to the whole, cohesive inner construction, dramatic wholeness, vivid characterization, climactic impact, all pervaded by rich and varied schemes of color. Color at times becomes the theme of his work, without, however, disturbing or destroying the integrity of the unity he demanded in his painting. In addition, we can be made aware that rhythms, patterns, and forms, with their relationships projecting a special kind of unity, can be a directing force in our mental life.

The foregoing are the prominences. Fused to them are the infinite variations of ideas, treatments, and personal approaches lying within the scope of the artist. The conversion of area into types of space, the projection of color into effects of light, the varied manipulations of painted surfaces having to do with texture are enrichments we may savor or allow to excite us. But the esthetic content actually arises from the character of the established order.

The consolidation of all his forms, components, and color into an acute single vision demonstrates Jonson's attempt to sublimate all aspects of his work in the hope of attaining a transcendent experience. The painting itself is an actual object, but within its substance there must be the creation of characteristics that will stimulate us to go beyond the concrete and the objective. We realize that a major intention of the concept of *design* is to create an enduring form that will project by implication the varieties of felt ideas. What we see is something that comes to us as a sensation, an emotion, rather than as a thing.

Design intensifies, beautifies, and demonstrates the ideal of order, so that its power will carry over into our living something vital, something higher than the ordinary aspects of life, something realizable in art and life. The esthetic experience cannot be merely an exterior observation or the recognition of that which is familiar to us, but must of necessity be an interior, spiritual, reviving encounter. Jonson saw this experience as a type of salvation.

It is an experience of something beyond what Jonson saw in modern society with its injustices, its anarchy, its frequent resort to war, its cycles of inflation and depression, its uncritical acceptance of ugliness and filth as concomitants of urban life, its imposition of price tags as the measure of human achievement. He searched for a realization in his life and art of that purity of expression he did not find in the world about him. To the corrupting influences of society he set up a constructive contrast to give direction to his creativity. To bring order out of the disorder of his times, to find in himself the creative force that could deny the social, political, warring chaos of the century in which he lived, he wanted the art of painting to function in opposition to all the forces of disunity and to express the harmony that seemed to him to be the world's need.

He wrote of placing "a new aspect and function on the creative arts." In a time of war he wrote to one of his many young friends:

So much can come between what one can do and what one actually does that we all need to look life squarely from the front. We often need to build up around us a kind of protective shell in order to keep out all those forces that hammer at us in a destructive way. We need to clarify our inner and outer life in such a way that expression can flow honestly, sincerely, and constructively.

America today faces the possibility of greatness and decline. The world, generally, is on the decline as we are sadly witnessing. Your generation has the terrific problem of keeping calm—loving and working out the program for living as brothers and not savages. In that program it will be necessary for some to express the soul—life—rhythms—vibrations which may form the historical statement of the age. . . .

Always during murder, hate, chaos, disorder, it is necessary that a few humans keep calm and work constructively. And I believe it best to work in an entirely different medium to that used by the haters. Right now we need works done that present a high state of order. They will not be seen by many but that does not matter for the act of doing releases that power, that sincerity and feeling that must have [their] effect. I realize this places a new aspect and function on the creative arts. I intend it to.[5]

If this revolutionary character of Jonson's art is missed, an important implication of his work is also missed. This meaning in Jonson's work does not parallel or sympathize with the tempestuous activities customarily associated with change. When those who claimed they spoke in the voice of revolution and peace indulged in violence, he rejected them. He abhorred violence as strongly as he did the things against which it was directed. His attitude has more nearly coincided with that of the leaders of our century whose antiviolent activity insists on telling us of an ideal rather than holding up a mirror to a world that is socially and politically grotesque. For Jonson it was not enough to reject. It was necessary for him to provide an affirmative view. He felt that "the function of the artist is to create or present something that is a statement of the finest qualities in the human mind and emotions."[6]

The form that Jonson chose for his statement moved it radically away from the problems of external reality and established, by a long process of self-definition, a meaning of its own. It incorporates Jonson's idealism, providing a holiday for the spirit and emotional release from the lowered values of routine life. It offers something not readily found in the day-to-day regularities of work and entertainment. If one can appreciate a Jonson painting with an understanding of his intentions, one can see it as an island of spiritual elevation. In those works of Jonson's that have appeared out of an inner requirement for order and harmony we find descriptions of ideal situations carried to the furthest limits of his capabilities for refinement.

It is a utopian world, a private world which we are asked to enter. We can learn from it by differentiating between whatever harmony may exist in the objective world and its happenings and the harmony of the painter's order which, in mastery, is absolute. We have observed Jonson's created world develop through various levels of abstracted order that may be seen and felt as a universal statement. It developed through a meticulously created environment in which there is a commitment to the hope that it might express the larger universe of the spirit.

The character of his work is organic, an emotional quality of purity capable of conveyance only through creative sincerity. It produces a beauty expressing the rapture of the unique experience and its delineation. It produces a beauty flowing from the interior regions of personality and instinct. It produces a beauty welling up from the intimate sources of freedom and life.

When Jonson wrote, "My life has been painting and painting has been my life,"[7] his meaning reached to more than one realizes. The unity between himself and his work was an essential requirement of his life as man and artist. The conviction of unity between the person and the act of life is not to make the act the expression of some special faculty but to make it an expression of the whole self.

Jonson makes his appeal to the whole person through the esthetic sense. He invites others to join him in the art with which he is concerned, an art depending primarily on visual sensibility and its attendant perceptions. It was his belief and his ideal that his business was to show the connection between visual sensibility and the rest of life.

Jonson found a vital link that drew painting and living together. In their union an art was produced that was indigenous to both. To the evanescence of individual life he linked the eternality of the formal qualities of art and found an equilibrium to which he gave expression. It is an equilibrium that he has brought to the works of his maturity, an equilibrium that can bring to those who experience his work a sense of peace, of life in balance wherein the "fusion of matter with spirit" is brought to fulfillment.

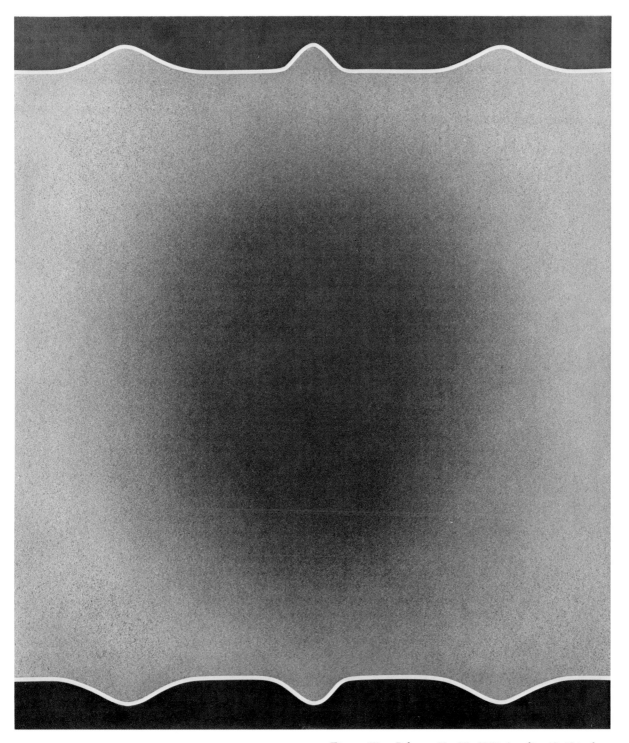

Figure 71. *Polymer No. 17—1974.* Acrylic, 48x42 inches.

Photograph by Eugene Hutchinson, Chicago, 1914.

Photograph by Helge Gilbert, Albuquerque, 1962.

Photograph by John Waggaman, Albuquerque, 1966.

Photograph by John Waggaman, Albuquerque, 1975.

Chronology

Beginning with 1910 are shown the works done each year that are still in existence as listed in the complete Jonson catalog.

1891   Born 18 July, the first of six children, to Reverend Gustav and Josephine Abrahamson Johnson on the farm of his maternal grandparents near Chariton, Iowa. His father, on coming to America from Sweden, had changed the spelling of his name from Jonsson to Johnson.

1899   Colorado Springs, Colorado. Attends school for the first time but previously had been taught to read and write by his mother.

1902   Portland, Oregon. Here ends family's peripatetic life occasioned by previous movements from church to church (Iowa, Minnesota, Wyoming, Colorado, Kansas) in the father's career as a preacher.

1909   Enrolls in newly opened art school at the Portland Art Museum, the first pupil to sign for enrollment.

1910   *2 student charcoal studies*
Moves to Chicago in September and enters the Chicago Academy of Fine Arts where he studies with, among others, Wellington J. Reynolds. To support himself takes various part-time jobs but spends all possible time on his studies and his rapidly expanding concepts of the meanings of art. A great event of October is Walter Brookins's flying exhibitions: "The first time anybody has flown in Chicago." Later enrolls at the Art Institute for classes in addition to those at the Academy.

1911   *2 student charcoal studies*
Continues with a full schedule of art classes and his part-time jobs. Feels increasing dissatisfaction with the commercial attitude toward art at the Academy and decides his future is to be in "real art."

1912   *5 oils; 2 student charcoal studies*
In May, with J. Blanding Sloan and Carl Oscar Erickson (Eric), acquires studio near Jackson Park. B. J. O. Nordfelt lives across the street, and a close but informal teacher-student association ensues.
Submits works for public exhibition for the first time. Two oils accepted at Wanamaker's in Philadelphia.

1913   *6 oils; 1 charcoal drawing; 1 etching*
The Armory Show comes to Chicago, a milestone in Jonson's life as a painter. Spends a summer month at home in Portland.
Joins the Chicago Little Theatre, founded by Maurice Browne and Ellen Van Volkenburg, as Graphic Arts Director, beginning his career as stage, costume, lighting designer, and sometimes actor. Designs sets for Yeats's *The Shadowy Waters*, Alice Brown's *Joint Owners in Spain*, and other plays. Exhibits three paintings in Third Annual Exhibition of Swedish-American Artists at the Swedish Club, his first showing in Chicago. *A Sun-kissed Mountain* included in the Twenty-Sixth Annual Exhibition of American Paintings and Sculpture at Chicago Art Institute.

1914   *5 oils*
Stage designs for Euripides' *Medea* and *The Trojan Women;* Shaw's *The Philanderer;* Dunsany's *The Lost Silk Hat.* In June has a three-week vacation in Iowa with his friend Lester Luther followed by sketching trip, July and August, in Texas, New Mexico, and Colorado with Blanding Sloan. Their automobile finally bogs down in Kansas mud.
Many theater works are included in Chicago Art Institute, An Exhibition of the New Stage Craft, 21 December to 10 January, 1915.
Exhibits *A City Canyon* in Eighteenth Annual Artists of Chicago and Vicinity Exhibition at Art Institute, and an etching, *South Twelfth Street,* with Chicago Society of Etchers also at the Art Institute. The University of Michigan Library has this etching, the only Jonson etching known to exist.

1915   *9 oils; 3 charcoal drawings*
Designs, among others, sets and costumes for Cloyd Head's *Grotesques;* Andreyev's *The Pretty Sabine Women;* and a new production of *The Trojan Women.* Nationwide tour of *The Trojan Women* gives opportunity for first California visit and a brief visit with his family in Portland. Exhibits three oils in Nineteenth Annual Artists of Chicago and Vicinity at Art Institute; two etchings with Chicago Society of Etchers at Art Institute; one-man exhibition of theater works at Chicago Little Theatre.

1916   *11 oils; 1 charcoal and pastel*
Designs sets and costumes for Shaw's *Mrs. Warren's Profession;* Browne's *King of the Jews;* Hankin's *The Charity That Began at Home;* and for

Menorah Society production of Horace Kallen's *Job, as a Greek Tragedy* at Harvard University.

Exhibits: Sixth Annual Exhibition of Swedish-American Artists in Chicago; forty-six stage works in "Exhibit of the Little Theatre" in St. Louis, Mo., for convention of The Drama League of America; four works in Midwest tour assembled by Carl Smalley.

Marries Vera White on 25 December, a marriage lasting until her death, 13 June 1965.

1917   *23 oils; 3 drawings*
Final season of the Chicago Little Theatre. Designs sets for new productions of *Medea* and Shaw's *The Philanderer,* and for Shaw's *Candida* and Synge's *Deirdre of the Sorrows.* Begins teaching at Chicago Academy of Fine Arts. With Vera spends a summer month in Portland followed by painting in September in Eldora, Colorado, which has a strong impact on his emotions and is an important influence on his work.

Exhibits: Seventh Annual Swedish-American Artists; Twenty-First Annual Artists of Chicago at Art Institute; at Grand Central Galleries, New York, in first Independent Society of Artists Exhibition. Is included in stagecraft exhibitions in Detroit and St. Louis, and has eighteen designs and models in "Retrospective Exhibition of Theatre Craft" at Arden Gallery, New York. Other exhibitions include Midwest travel exhibition assembled by Carl Smalley; "Independent Exhibition," Arts Club, Chicago; "Fourteen Chicago Painters" at Aeolian Hall.

First one-man exhibition is at University of Wisconsin, Madison and consists of thirty-one paintings and drawings, thirty-five designs for the theater, and four stage models.

1918   *16 oils; 6 drawings*
Starts his diary at beginning of this year; continues to 1926.
In February Midwest tour with Rolf and Borgny Hammer in Ibsen's *Hedda Gabler* and *The Master Builder.* Tour then extends to Wyoming, Utah, and Idaho until March. Living and painting in Utah and Estes Park, Colorado, until 1 May.

Exhibits: Twenty-Second Annual Artists of Chicago and Thirty-First Annual American Exhibitions at Art Institute, with "The Independents" at Chicago Arts Club, and in three Carl Smalley Midwest tours. Four works at Museum of New Mexico, Santa Fe; his first showing there. University of Oklahoma Museum of Art purchases *Irony,* Jonson's first sale to a museum.

1919   *17 oils; 4 temperas; 1 watercolor; 2 drawings*
In February resigns from teaching at Chicago Academy of Fine Arts but returns in April.

John Cowper Powys lectures on Jonson's art in Chicago. Receives New York City MacDowell Association scholarship to MacDowell Colony at Peterborough, N.H. Beginning of friendship with poets Edwin Arlington Robinson and John Curtis Underwood. Ten of the oil sketches and three paintings done at Peterborough included in above total of surviving oils. After closing of MacDowell Colony in the autumn, remains for three weeks in Peterborough, then goes to Boston and New York to see museums and galleries. Returns to Chicago in early November.

Exhibits: Twenty-Third Annual Artists of Chicago at Art Institute; Eighth Annual Swedish-Amercan Artists Exhibition, Chicago; "American Stage Designs" at Bourgeois Gallery, New York. Spends month of December in Portland following death of his father in an automobile accident in late November. On way back to Chicago visits the Brownes at Nellita on Puget Sound.

Changes spelling of name from Johnson to Jonson.

1920　*24 oils; 7 drawings*

In New York for production of Euripides' *Medea* at Garrick Theater for which he designs the set and costumes and acts as stage manager. At close goes to Ogunquit, Maine, 29 April until 17 May. Fifteen oil sketches and four drawings survive. Series of sea paintings, 1921–23, result from this visit. To MacDowell Colony until 16 July. Seven oil sketches survive.

At Grand Haven, Michigan, and Lake Forest, Illinois, until 1 September.

Exhibits: Twenty-Fourth Annual Artists of Chicago at Art Institute (*Silent Spaces* given Honorable Mention); Ninth Annual Swedish-American Artists Exhibition (catalog cover designed by Jonson); exhibition assembled in New York shown in Göteborg, Malmö, and Stockholm, Sweden, National Academy of Design, New York, and Chicago Art Institute.

Invited to show at Mississippi Art Association, Jackson. Association purchases *Mountain Vista*.

1921　*14 oils; 9 drawings*

Teaches stagecraft at Grace Hickox Studios, Chicago, and has one-man exhibition (fifty-eight works) there.

Meets Nicholas Roerich. "I feel very close and am moved beyond words by this man's spirit—his work."

Helps organize "Cor Ardens," planned to be a world organization of artists.

Sees the Eddy Collection and is especially moved by Kandinsky, though "not disturbed," and by Albert Bloch, who becomes a friend.

Once more makes "final resignation" from the faculty of Chicago Academy of Fine Arts.

Reads Kandinsky's *The Art of Spiritual Harmony* and is deeply affected by it.

Exhibits: Twenty-Fifth Annual Artists of Chicago at Art Institute; Tenth Annual Swedish-American Artists Exhibition (*The Night* awarded second prize).

Rejections by jury of Thirty-Fourth Annual American Exhibition at Art Institute leads to organization, largely by members of "Cor Ardens," of "Salon des Refusés."

1922   *39 oils; 5 watercolors; 5 drawings*
One-man exhibitions at Minneapolis Institute of Arts; Springfield (Illinois) Art Association; Cedar Rapids (Iowa) Art Association; Milwaukee Art Center; Madison (Wisconsin) Art Association; and Minnesota State Fair at Hamline. Exhibits nine works in International Stagecraft Exhibition in Amsterdam and London
"Cor Ardens" has its first, and last, exhibitions at the Arts Club of Chicago and Milwaukee Art Center.
Beginning in June Jonsons spend four months in Santa Fe, New Mexico, decide on it as their future home, and buy ground on which to build their residence and studio. In Santa Fe renews his contact with Nordfeldt. Of eighty-five sketches made during the summer, thirty-four oils and four watercolors survive.

1923   *4 oils*
Dedicates the year to a campaign to acquire funds needed for the move to and building of a home and studio in Santa Fe. Resumes teaching at Chicago Academy of Fine Arts.
Winter awarded Englewood Women's Club Prize at Twenty-Seventh Annual Artists of Chicago Exhibition at Art Institute. Charles Morris sees the exhibition and seeks out Jonson; a lifelong friendship, of highest importance to Jonson, ensues.
Sea Patterns shown in Eleventh Annual Swedish-American Exhibition in Chicago and sent to Tercentenary Exhibition in Göteborg, Sweden, where it receives good notice.
One-man exhibitions in Chicago at Hickox Studios and Walden Book Shop. One work in Chicago No-Jury Exhibition.

1924
Arrives in Santa Fe on 31 July. Sets to work building home. No painting done during the year.
One-man exhibitions at Omaha Society of Fine Arts; Kansas City (Missouri) Art Institute; Museum of New Mexico, Santa Fe. At last of these has had fifteen one-man exhibitions. Seven works in exhibition at University of Kansas Museum.

1925   *13 oils; 29 watercolors; 3 drawings*
Moves into new home and studio in Santa Fe.
Corona Mundi, International Art Center, later Riverside Museum, purchases *Earth Rhythms No. 1*, transferred to the Rose Art Museum, Brandeis University, in 1971.
The Power of God is awarded the Underwood Purchase Prize ($1,000) at Museum of New Mexico exhibition and *Light* purchased for the museum's permanent collection.
Meets Arnold Ronnebeck, "one person who gets what I'm aiming at."
At end of year decides not to submit to juries in future.

1926   *16 oils; 3 watercolors; 11 drawings*
Shows twenty-two watercolors in exhibitions in Tulsa and Chickasha, Oklahoma, and University of Kansas, Lawrence.
Earth Rhythms No. 5 invited to Philadelphia Sesquicentennial International Exposition Exhibition.
Opens his Atalaya Art School for teaching a ten-week summer session. Pupils' work exhibited at Museum of New Mexico.

1927   *11 oils; 23 drawings*
Six Men, exhibition group, organizes in Santa Fe: Andrew Dasburg, B. J. O. Nordfeldt, Joseph G. Bakos, Willard Nash, John E. Thompson, and Jonson.
East-West Gallery, San Francisco, opens with large exhibition by the Six Men group.
Organizes "Modern Wing" at Museum of New Mexico for monthly exhibitions by Six Men plus Russell Cowles and Olive Rush. Others invited to show from time to time. "Modern Wing" held thirty-two exhibitions until its discontinuance in 1931.
Visits the Grand Canyon and paints the first of his trilogies, based on sketches made at the canyon. Visits Carlsbad Caverns and in 1928 paints another trilogy based on the material sketched there.
Earth Rhythms No. 5 invited to "Selected American Paintings" exhibition at Albright Gallery, Buffalo, N.Y.
Vera starts working at Spanish and Indian Trading Company organized by Nordfeldt, Andrew Dasburg, Witter Bynner, and John Evans to deal in authentic native arts and crafts.
At end of summer discontinues Atalaya Art School. Sells first Santa Fe residence and plans building of new place nearby.

1928   *13 oils; 7 drawings*
Six Men exhibit at Henry Gallery, University of Washington, Seattle; Los Angeles County Museum; Tucson Fine Arts Association.
One-man exhibitions (forty works) at Houston Museum of Fine Arts in

February and University of Oklahoma Museum of Art in March. Shows nine drawings and two watercolors in "The Southwest" exhibition at California Palace of the Legion of Honor, San Francisco.
New residence and studio occupied in July.

1929   *20 oils; 1 watercolor; 4 drawings*
Brother Arthur and his wife, May Van Dyke, spend two summer months in Santa Fe.

1930   *19 oils; 12 watercolors; 10 drawings*
Growth Variant No. I exhibited in Salons of America at Anderson Galleries, New York.

1931   *10 oils; 21 drawings*
Exhibits *Variations on a Rhythm—A* at Henry Gallery, University of Washington, Seattle, under title "Abstract A" and in San Francisco Art Association Annual at California Palace of the Legion of Honor under title "Apex."
One-man exhibition at Delphic Studios, New York.
Visits New York.

1932   *18 oils; 5 drawings*
One-man exhibition at Studio Gallery of Increase Robinson, Chicago, in January. Another, consisting of drawings, at same gallery in May.
Renaissance Society at University of Chicago exhibits *Time Cycle: Morning, Noon, Night.*
Visits Chicago, New York, and Barnes Foundation at Merion, Pennsylvania.

1933   *12 oils; 7 watercolors; 34 drawings*
Variations on a Rhythm—I invited to exhibition, "Abstractions," at California Palace of the Legion of Honor, San Francisco, followed by showings at the Oakland and Honolulu museums.
Three-person exhibition: Agnes Pelton, Cady Wells, and Raymond Jonson at Museum of New Mexico, Santa Fe.
Visits Chicago and spends twenty days studying the Century of Progress art exhibition.

1934   *10 oils; 4 watercolors; 13 drawings*
Paints *A Cycle of Science,* six large "murals" for the University of New Mexico Library at Albuquerque.
Begins teaching one day a week at the university, commuting from Santa Fe.
Five works in exhibition touring the Pacific Coast.

1935   *24 oils; 1 watercolor; 5 drawings*
Abstraction in Red is invited to San Diego Pacific International Exposition

and *Suspended Figuration* to First Annual Artists West of the Mississippi Exhibition at Colorado Springs Fine Arts Center.

In December visits California; goes to Cathedral City to meet Agnes Pelton, for whose work he had great admiration.

1936   *12 oils; 3 watercolors; 17 drawings*
Art and *Science*, each 60 x 90 inches, installed at Eastern New Mexico University, Portales.

Exhibits at Rockefeller Center, New York, Denver Art Museum, and Putzel Gallery, Hollywood.

1937   *14 oils; 8 watercolors; 3 drawings*
One-man exhibition at Tulsa Art Center, Oklahoma. Other exhibitions at Las Vegas, New Mexico; Norfolk, Virginia, Museum of Arts and Sciences; Delgado Museum, New Orleans; Denver Art Museum; and Eliot O'Hara's Watercolor Gallery at Goose Rocks Beach, Maine. Last of these goes on year-long national tour.

Visits Tulsa and is judge for Eighth Annual Exhibition of Oklahoma artists. In December visits Chicago; visit extends into 1938.

In Chicago sees Archipenko exhibition, meets Archipenko and Moholy-Nagy. In letter to Vera dated 14 December 1937 he wrote:

> I am getting much from this trip. I hope to feel that a fresh impulse will result. The geometrical painters such as Albers, Moholy-Nagy, Helion, etc. have gone so much farther in the purity of form that my exhibit will probably look a little academic! But I do not quite agree with the geometrical approach and feel confident that my own can go farther in the end than the other. But at present . . . it is farther along the path than the thing I am after.

1938   *3 oils; 6 temperas; 32 watercolors*
Abandons practice of giving titles to his works and, with few exceptions, uses medium-number-year designation hereafter.

In Chicago has one-man exhibition at Katharine Kuh Gallery. In Santa Fe joins faculty of Arsuna, school of fine arts. Begins use of airbrush for temperas and watercolors.

Nine artists—Raymond Jonson, Bill Lumpkins, Emil Bisttram, Robert Gribbroek, Lawren Harris, Florence Miller (Pierce), Agnes Pelton, H. Towner Pierce, and Stuart Walker—organize the Transcendental Painting Group, "composed of artists who are concerned with the development and presentation of various types of nonrepresentational painting." Jonson is chairman and Lumpkins is secretary-treasurer.

Jonson sees painting by Ed Garman at home of mutual friend, Howard

Schleeter, seeks out Garman and begins lifelong friendship. In 1941 Garman becomes the only additional member of the Transcendental Painting Group.

1939 *9 oils; 1 oil and tempera; 2 temperas; 23 watercolors*
Transcendental Painting Group is invited to exhibit together at Golden Gate International Exposition, San Francisco, and has exhibitions at Museum of New Mexico, Santa Fe, and University of New Mexico, Albuquerque.

1940 *8 oils; 6 oil and temperas; 9 temperas; 30 watercolors*
Exhibits with Transcendental Painting Group at Guggenheim Museum, New York.

1941 *11 oils; 2 oil and temperas; 10 temperas; 28 watercolors*
"Painters of New Mexico" exhibition tours California: Santa Barbara, Los Angeles, Sacramento, Stockton.
One-man exhibition at The University of New Mexico contains thirty-seven works. At New Mexico State Fair *Crystal* awarded "Grand Champion" prize, best work in all classes and mediums.
Watercolor No. 9—1940 in State Museum tour exhibited in Minneapolis, Kansas City, Tulsa, Philadelphia, Rochester, and Boston; tour extending into 1942.

1942 *12 oils; 1 oil and tempera; 8 temperas; 30 watercolors*
One-man exhibition, Martha White Memorial Gallery, Santa Fe.
Has five works in university faculty tour with twenty showings through Midwest.

1943 *10 oils; 4 temperas; 37 watercolors*
Society for Contemporary American Art invites *Casein Tempera No. 1—1940* to its exhibition at Chicago Art Institute.

1944 *6 oils; 3 temperas; 40 watercolors*
Chaffey Community Art Association, Ontario, California invites two works for its annual exhibition.

1945 *11 oils; 41 watercolors*
Los Angeles County Museum First Biennial Exhibition of Drawings includes three by Jonson.
Cincinnati Art Museum exhibition, the Critics' Choice of Contemporary American Painting, shows *1942*.

1946 *20 oils; 3 temperas; 25 watercolors*
One-man exhibition at Pat Wall Gallery, Monterey, California.
Two works are in Philadelphia Art Alliance exhibition: Artists of Santa Fe; also shown at Ball State College, Muncie, Indiana.
Delta Phi Delta, national art fraternity, elects Jonson a laureate member.

1947   *15 oils; 1 tempera; 1 gouache; 24 watercolors*
First steps taken toward founding of Jonson Gallery at The University of New Mexico.
Oil No. 1—1946 invited to Colorado Springs Fine Arts Center Ninth Annual Artists West of the Mississippi; *Casein Tempera No. 2—1944* to Dallas Museum of Fine Arts exhibition: Six Southwestern States; and *Watercolor No. 3—1945 (Green Environment)* to Chicago Art Institute Fifty-Eighth Annual American Exhibition: Abstract and Surrealist American Art.

1948   *1 oil; 1 tempera; 2 gouaches; 30 watercolors*
Three-man exhibition: John Skolle, Ed Garman, Raymond Jonson at Museum of New Mexico, Santa Fe.
One-man retrospective (1918–48) exhibition at Fine Arts Gallery, University of New Mexico.
Planning and financing of Jonson Gallery proceeds.

1949   *6 oils; 1 watercolor; 11 drawings*
Begins full-time teaching at University of New Mexico with rank of professor, and Jonsons move to Albuquerque.
Eleven small ink drawings executed this year are illustrations for Winter issue of New Mexico Quarterly, which also has article on Jonson by Ben Wolf.
One-man exhibition at New Mexico Highlands University, Las Vegas.
Jonson Gallery under construction.

1950   *18 watercolors*
Jonson Gallery—The University of New Mexico opens on January 8 with thirty-eight-year retrospective exhibition consisting of thirty paintings.

1951   *7 oils; 11 watercolors*

1952   *13 oils; 3 watercolors*
Exhibits three works in Internationale Graphik exhibition at Salzburg, Austria, also shown at Secession Gallery, Vienna.

1953   *16 oils; 9 watercolors; 3 drawings*
Three-man exhibition: Frederick O'Hara, Howard B. Schleeter, Raymond Jonson at Modern Museum, Albuquerque.

1954   *16 oils; 20 temperas; 2 watercolors*
Becomes emeritus professor of art but continues as director of Jonson Gallery.
Cincinnati Art Museum shows *Oil No. 10—1953* at Colorado Springs Fine Art Center exhibition: New Accessions, U.S.A.

1955   *30 oils; 25 temperas*

1956   *21 oils; 32 temperas*
School of American Research elects Jonson an honorary fellow.
One-man retrospective (1912–56) exhibition of seventy-eight works at
Museum of New Mexico, Santa Fe.

1957   *24 oils; 6 polymers; 17 drawings*
Drawing No. 1–1953 in exhibition, Golden Years of American Drawing at
Brooklyn Museum. Exhibits in First (January) and Second (October)
Invitational Exhibitions at New Mexico Highlands University, Las Vegas.
Begins using "Liquitex" acrylic polymer medium.

1958   *16 oils; 31 polymers*

1959   *5 oils; 30 polymers*

1960   *15 oils; 18 polymers*
One-man exhibition at Roswell Museum and Art Center which acquires *Oil
No. 21–1956* to start its Jonson collection. Great Jones Gallery, New York,
exhibits thirteen Albuquerque artists including Jonson.

1961   *27 polymers*
Polymer No. 24–1959 in exhibition, West Comes East, at Newman
Galleries, Philadelphia, and six works in Sixth Annual Invitational at New
Mexico Highlands University, Las Vegas.

1962   *55 polymers*

1963   *23 polymers*
Two works in exhibition: Taos and Santa Fe: The Artist's Environment,
shown at Amon Carter Museum of Western Art, Fort Worth, Texas; La
Jolla (California) Museum of Art; and as the opening exhibition at new
University of New Mexico Art Museum.

1964   *57 polymers*
One-man retrospective (1918–64) exhibition of sixty-nine works at University of New Mexico Art Museum.

1965   *30 polymers; 3 lithographs*
Vera Jonson dies June 13. On August 24 Jonson wrote to Ed Garman:

> This has been a very difficult period in my life. To go into detail
> would accomplish nothing for I must work through this desolation by myself. But so far have made little headway. Nevertheless, in spite of strain and many ordinary duties have with terrific
> will power and necessity brought to conclusion the first work
> since Vera's death. I was in hopes that it would not be a sad or
> tragic result. It is not.

Archives of American Art, now at Smithsonian Institution, Washington, D.C., microfilms Jonson documents, manuscripts, catalog, photographs of works, and correspondence on ten microfilm rolls.

In autumn brother Arthur moves permanently to Albuquerque. President of the university appoints him curator of Jonson Gallery.

Vera Jonson Memorial Collection of twenty-nine items from her personal collection is established at Maxwell Museum of Anthropology, the University of New Mexico.

1966   *48 polymers*
Rising Tondo by Ilya Bolotowsky is acquired by University of New Mexico Art Museum through gifts of her friends as first work entering the Vera Jonson Memorial Collection.

1967   *25 polymers*
One-man exhibition of early works (1918–30) at Roswell Museum and Art Center.
Earth Rhythms No. 10 (1927) in exhibition, Cubism: Its Impact in the U.S.A., at University of New Mexico Art Museum; Marion Koogler McNay Art Institute, San Antonio, Texas; San Francisco Museum of Art; Los Angeles Municipal Art Gallery.

1968   *38 polymers; 1 drawing*
Exhibits *Polymer No. 18—1966* in New Mexico Invitational Exhibition at Museum of New Mexico, Santa Fe.

1969   *39 polymers*

1970   *39 polymers*
Polymer No. 13—1959 in exhibition, Masterpieces from the Museum of New Mexico, at Marion Koogler McNay Art Institute, San Antonio, Texas; also shown at Museum of New Mexico.
Exhibition, Lure of the West, at Salt Lake Art Center, Utah, includes six Jonson paintings.

1971   *28 polymers*
One-man exhibition at Hill's Gallery, Santa Fe is inaugural exhibition of the gallery.
The University of New Mexico confers honorary degree, Doctor of Humane Letters.

> Master-painter, teacher at the University for more than 20 years, and founder and director of the Jonson Gallery, his life and works are a celebration of the human spirit, a triumphant assertion of the power of contemporary ideas in art. Represented in 46 museums and other public collections, he has been a continuing

source of inspiration to generations of younger painters in New Mexico, and his originality and contagious enthusiasm for his art have served as a powerful counter-force to provincialism. Since his retirement from active teaching 17 years ago, his productivity and commitment to his work have never faltered, and he has continued to give generously of his time to all who would learn. The history of art in New Mexico is enriched by his contribution.

1972 *26 polymers*
Exhibits in opening exhibition of Greenhill Galleries at Fort Lauderdale, Florida.
Receives grant from National Endowment for the Arts.

1973 *25 polymers*
Exhibits six works in 1973 Fall Invitational at Roswell Museum and Art Center.

1974 *30 polymers*
Denver Art Museum includes two works by Jonson (borrowed from collections in Denver and Santa Fe) in Picturesque Images from Taos and Santa Fe exhibition.
Twenty-Fifth Anniversary Exhibition at Jonson Gallery—UNM shows three-part retrospective totaling sixty-seven works (1913–74):
Drawn and Painted in New Mexico exhibition (two paintings) and a Performing Arts Exhibition (nine theater designs) at the University of New Mexico Art Museum.

Public Collections

Works in all media are included. Collections which contain more than one work have the number of works shown in parentheses.

Amon Carter Museum of Western Art, Fort Worth, Texas, (3)
Arizona State University Art Collections, Tempe (2)
University of Arkansas, Fayetteville
Augustana Hospital, Chicago, Illinois
Boise Gallery of Art, Idaho (7)
University of British Columbia, Vancouver
Cincinnati Art Museum, Ohio
University of Cincinnati, Ohio
City of Chicago Municipal Collection, Illinois
College of Santa Fe, New Mexico (2)
Dallas Museum of Fine Arts, Texas
Eastern New Mexico University, Portales (3)
Elvehjem Art Center, University of Wisconsin, Madison
Encyclopaedia Britannica Collection, Chicago, Illinois
Grunwald Graphic Arts Foundation, University of California, Los Angeles (3)
University of Kansas Museum of Art, Lawrence
La Jolla Museum of Art, California
La Mesa School, Albuquerque, New Mexico
Los Angeles County Museum, California (3)
Louisiana State University, Baton Rouge
MacDowell Society of Evanston, Illinois
Marion Koogler McNay Art Institute, San Antonio, Texas
University of Michigan Library, Ann Arbor (11)

Milwaukee Art Center, Wisconsin (2)
University of Minnesota Art Gallery, Minneapolis
Mississippi Art Association, Jackson
Museum of Modern Art, New York, New York (3)
Museum of Navajo Ceremonial Art, Santa Fe, New Mexico
Museum of New Mexico, Museum of Fine Arts, Santa Fe (17)
University of New Mexico Art Museum, Albuquerque (16)
College of Education, University of New Mexico, Albuquerque
Oklahoma Art Center, Oklahoma City
Oklahoma State University, Stillwater
University of Oklahoma Museum of Art, Norman (3)
University of Oregon Museum of Art, Eugene (2)
Portland Art Museum, Oregon (6)
Rose Art Museum, Brandeis University, Waltham, Massachusetts (3)
Roswell Museum and Art Center, New Mexico (14)
Salt Lake Art Center, Salt Lake City, Utah (2)
Santa Barbara Museum of Art, California
Sheldon Memorial Art Gallery, University of Nebraska, Lincoln
Smokey Hill Art Club, Lindsborg, Kansas
Southern Colorado State College, Pueblo
Texas Agricultural and Mechanical University, College Station
Texas Technological University Art Institute, Lubbock
University of Texas, Austin
University of Tulsa, Oklahoma
Vanderpoel Memorial Collection, Chicago, Illinois (2)
William Rockhill Nelson Gallery of Art, Kansas City, Missouri

Notes

Prologue

1. These five quotations are from:
   Jonson to his family, 18 November 1912, Jonson letters.
   Diary, 11 November 1918, Jonson Gallery archives.
   Diary, 20 April 1921, Jonson Gallery archives
   Jonson to Charles Morris, January 1938, Jonson letters.
   Jonson to Ben Wolf, 28 October 1949, Jonson letters.

1. Introduction

1. Catalog, Hill's Gallery, Santa Fe. *An Exhibition of Paintings by Raymond Jonson.* 4 April–5 May 1971.

2. L. C. [Lawrence Campbell], "Fourteen Albuquerque Painters," *Art News,* February 1960, p. 18.

3. Citation, Doctor of Humane Letters degree for Raymond Jonson. The University of New Mexico, 6 June 1971.

4. The modern movement was institutionalized in 1929 and 1930 with the founding of the Museum of Modern Art and the Whitney Museum of American Art in New York. Stieglitz had exhibited Rodin and Matisse as early as 1908, and the Armory Show in 1913 had galvanized public attention. Ortega y Gasset, in an important criticism, *The Dehumanization of Art,* considered 1925 as the year in which the modern movement had reached a culmination, so that it could no longer be called seminal.

5. Among the artists who preceded Jonson in Santa Fe were William Penhallow Henderson (1916), Andrew Dasburg (1917), B. J. O. Nordfeldt (1918), Willard Nash (1920), of whom only Henderson remained a permanent resident. Many artists of a more or less modern persuasion visited Santa Fe but contributed little, if anything, to the art life of the community as such.

6. The physical plant consists of a two-story building containing on the upper street level the gallery entrance, living quarters, and a "museum room." On the lower level which, due to the conformation of the site, is also at ground level, there are the main gallery, Jonson's studio, his office, two work shops, four storerooms, and a heating room.

7. In addition to the gifts by the Jonsons, Frank C. Rand, Jr., and Adele Levis Rand, were other contributions by Amelia Elizabeth White, Cady Wells, Mr. and Mrs. James G. McNary, Miss Margery McNary, and Mr. and Mrs. Earl Manning Oren.

8. The Jonson Gallery collections, as of 1 January 1975 are (1) the Jonson Reserved Retrospective Collection: 670 works in all mediums; (2) Other Artists' Works Collection: 493 works; (3) Student Works from Jonson's Classes: 326 works. Originally there was also a collection of arts and crafts consisting largely of Indian artifacts, most of which are now in the Vera Jonson Memorial Collection at the Maxwell Museum of Anthropology–The University of New Mexico.

9. "Jonson is probably the factor most responsible for encouraging the large amount of work and high level of professionalism of the young Albuquerque artists (most of them in their middle thirties) by offering them one-man shows at his gallery. Without this goad, many of them feel they might have become too discouraged to go on in a vacuum" (Elaine de Kooning, "New Mexico," *Art in America* 49, no. 4, p. 56).

10. Ina Sizer Cassidy, "The Raymond Jonson Gallery," *New Mexico Magazine* 28, no. 3 (March 1950).

11. Jonson to his sister Ruth, 8 June 1920, Jonson letters.

12. *Diary*, n.d. (between 7 and 16 July 1920), Jonson Gallery archives.

13. Ibid.

2. Beginnings

1. Arthur Johnson to Ed Garman, 13 October 1959.

2. Sam Hunter, *Modern American Painting and Sculpture* (New York: Dell Publishing Co., 1959).

3. Alfred Werner, "Max Weber at Seventy-Seven," *Arts Magazine*, September 1958, p. 27.

4. Catalog. Art School, Portland Art Association, 1910–11.

3. Sense of Mission

1. Arthur Johnson to Ed Garman, 13 October 1959.

2. Jonson talk to the Chili Club, Santa Fe, N.M., 29 August 1949.

4. The Chicago Academy of Fine Arts

1. Jonson to his family, 8 October 1910, Jonson letters.

2. Ibid.

3. Joaquín Sorolla, a Spanish painter, was visiting instructor at the art school of the Art Institute of Chicago in 1910–11. The institute's *Guide to the Paintings in the Permanent Collection*, 1925, says of Sorolla, "He painted broadly, with forceful finality, filling his canvases with the warmth of sunlight."

5. "The Little Studio"

1. Jonson to his family 31 January 1913, Jonson letters.

2. Jonson to his family, 12 May 1912, Jonson letters.

3. J. Blanding Sloan moved on to New York, then to California. He was, like Jonson, a stage designer and for a time ran a little theater in San Francisco. He too has continued as a painter. Carl Oscar Erickson was to become the famous Eric of *Vogue*.

4. Mary O'Connor Newell, "Chicago's Little Parnassus," Chicago *Sunday Record-Herald*, 10 November 1912.

5. Jonson to his family, 18 November 1912, Jonson letters.

6. *Old Woman* is one of twenty-three Nordfeldt works in the Jonson Collection–The University of New Mexico (Other Artists' Works) at Jonson Gallery.

7. In 1956 at the request of the author Jonson sent him a lengthy, undated memorandum about his association with Nordfeldt from which the quotation has been extracted.

6. Growth

1. Louis H. Sullivan, *Kindergarten Chats* (New York: Wittenborg, Schultz, c. 1947), p. 206.

2. Harriet Monroe, *Chicago Tribune*. 17 March 1912. Quoted by Frederick S. Wight in the catalog *Arthur G. Dove* (Berkeley and Los Angeles, University of California Press, 1958), p. 30.

3. George Cram Cook, *Chicago Evening Post Literary Review*. 29 March 1912. Quoted in Wight, *Dove*, p. 32.

4. Jonson witnessed this caper. "They used an old mattress."

5. Walt Kuhn in *The Story of the Armory Show* (1938) says it was a sixth toe.

6. Catalog, Munson-Williams-Proctor Institute, Utica, N.Y. *1913 Armory Show 50th Anniversary Exhibition, 1963*.

7. "Raymond Jonson, then an art student in Chicago, was deeply affected by this exhibition and was one of the few in the Chicago area who felt its true significance. In fact, he was almost alone in his response. I learned this recently from Beatrice Levy, painter and graphic artist of national reputation, who was a contemporary of Mr. Jonson's in Chicago. She spoke of the many years when he worked practically in isolation, as he adopted and contributed to the development of this new conception for the visual arts, which he eventually fashioned through his own efforts into a unique and personal artistic expression" (Frederick O'Hara, "Modern Art Today," *El Palacio* 63, nos. 5–6 (May–June 1956):132, 134.

8. Jonson to his mother, 24 March 1913, Jonson letters.

7. The Chicago Little Theatre

1. Jonson to his mother, 30 March 1913, Jonson letters.

2. Maurice Browne, *Too Late to Lament* (London: Victor Gollancz, 1955; Bloomington: Indiana University Press, 1956), p. 122. Browne's account does not agree with Jonson's in the previously quoted letter written at the time in which he says it was Lou Wall Moore, in whose studio the group was rehearsing, who brought him in. However, Nordfeldt, also a neighbor, designed the stage for the Little Theatre's first production of *The Trojan Women* in January 1913, for which Mrs. Moore designed the costumes. Browne undoubtedly consulted with Nordfeldt as to the proposed engagement of his young pupil. Considering the nature of Jonson's letters to his parents in which he expresses so many doubts and frustrations, Nordfeldt's alleged remark, "thinking that he knew everything," seems unlikely and is probably a Browne embellishment.

3. Jonson to Ed Garman, 18 September 1956, Jonson letters.

4. In *Homecoming, An Autobiography* (New York: Farrar and Rinehart, 1933), p. 223, Floyd Dell wrote: "The Little Theatre which Maurice Browne started, up in the top of a building on

Michigan Boulevard, opened with a play of Yeats's "On Baile's Strand" and I was enchanted with Raymond Jonson's deep grave voice as Conchobar or Cuchulein, I forget which, I think the former; and some of the speeches of the play have stayed in my mind to this day." The quotation is given in order to correct its misinformation, as Dell was in error. It was not Raymond Jonson who so impressed Dell in *On Baile's Strand*, for he was not in the cast, and the actor Dell was remembering was Arthur Johnson (not Raymond Jonson's brother).

5. One wonders how much of the poet Yeats struck a sympathetic chord in Jonson since there are Yeatsian implications in some of his feelings concerning art. In *The Shadowy Waters*, a play contrasting two ways of love, the physical and metaphysical, the character Forgael says:

> For it is love that I am seeking for,
> But of a beautiful, unheard-of kind
> That is not in the world.

And in "Sailing to Byzantium," Yeats wrote:

> Once out of nature I shall never take
> My bodily form from any natural thing.

6. The Art Institute of Chicago. Catalogue of an Exhibition of the New Stage Craft, from 21 December 1914 to 10 January 1915.

7. Jonson to his family, 26 December 1914, Jonson letters.

8. Browne, *Too Late to Lament*. Again one must regretfully record an inaccuracy on Browne's part in that several American designers other than the three he names were included in the exhibition. Actually, there were twenty-seven stage models by eight designers and a large number of photographs, sketches, and reproductions of theater works by many European as well as American designers.

9. Bourgeois Galleries, New York. *American Stage Designs*. Catalog, 5–26 April 1919. Reprinted in *Theatre Arts Magazine* 3, no. 2 (April 1919):121.

10. Abstracted from the typescript of a colloquy in December 1966 between Jonson and Edward R. Kesner prepared for Jerrold A. Phillips, New York University.

11. Harriet Monroe published the text of Cloyd Head's *Grotesques* in the October 1916 issue of *Poetry: A Magazine of Verse*. In a note on the production, she wrote:

> An enthusiastic word should be added for the beauty of Mr. Raymond Jonson's part of the production. Scenically this play was a new and difficult problem, whose fit solution required a man of daring vision and delicate instinct for line and balance in decorative design. In many earlier Little Theatre productions Mr. Jonson had shown rare ability and originality as a scenic designer, as well as extraordinary taste and ingenuity in producing new and strange effects with fixed or changing lights. *Grotesques* might have been ruined by a scenic artist less sensitive to conventionalized rhythms in background, costumes, and the posing of figures.

12. Eunice Tietjens. *Theatre Arts Magazine* 4, no. 3 (July 1920):227–37 (with five reproductions).

13. Jonson to his mother, 11 September 1916, Jonson letters.

14. Jonson to his mother, 1 November 1913, Jonson letters.

15. Maurice Block, *Omaha Evening World Herald*, 7 April 1924.

16. *Minneapolis Journal*, (no by-line), 8 January 1922.

17. Jonson met John Curtis Underwood at the MacDowell Colony in 1919 to begin a friendship that lasted until the poet's death. Underwood, who had a home in Santa Fe, was instrumental in the Jonson move to New Mexico. He purchased a number of works, including *Light*, which he gave to the Museum of New Mexico, and *The Power of God*. The latter is now in the Jonson Retrospective Collection–The University of New Mexico, presented to the collection by Mrs. Underwood as a memorial to her late husband.

18. Jonson talk to the Chili Club of Santa Fe, 16 December 1946.

19. Jonson to Ed Garman, December 26, 1957, Jonson letters.

8. The MacDowell Colony

1. *Diary*, 16 April 1919, Jonson Gallery archives.

2. *Diary*, 28 December 1920, Jonson Gallery archives.

3. *Diary*, added to an entry for 16 October 1920 and dated only December, Jonson Gallery archives.

4. *Diary*, 18, February 1921, Jonson Gallery archives.

5. *The Sea* is at Augustana Hospital, Chicago, and *Age* in the collection of Mrs. Mollie Salmon, Chicago.

9. Declaration of Purpose

1. Jonson to his sister Esther, 23 September 1916, Jonson letters.

2. *Diary*, 27 January 1918, Jonson Gallery archives.

3. Jonson to his brother Arthur, 29 February 1932, Jonson letters.

4. Jonson to Charles Morris, 19 March 1932, Jonson letters.

5. Jonson to Charles Morris, 6 June 1939, Jonson letters.

6. Jonson to his brother Arthur, 31 December 1940, Jonson letters.

11. Influences

1. Essential form is something that is a necessity in the characterization of the subject. It is a part of the actuality of the subject, and yet it is something that can be transformed into an art form; something of such great vitality that, although it is transformed into an art form, it remains relevant to its original context. And though in its new identity it remains as only a faint echo of its original and former self, it still comes through forcefully and distinctively.

2. Clive Bell, *Art* (New York: Frederick A. Stokes, n.d. [Bell's preface is dated November 1913]), pp. 220, 223, 228–29.

3. *Diary*, 21 July 1919 and 10 August 1919, Jonson Gallery archives.

4. *Diary*, entry undated. The context suggests July 1920.

5. *Diary*, 20 April 1921, Jonson Gallery archives.

6. Kandinsky's *On the Spiritual in Art* was published in 1911. The first English edition, called *The Art of Spiritual Harmony*, was published in 1914. Jonson's first copy was a gift from Sheldon Cheney. It was lost or stolen, and Vera bought him the Houghton Mifflin edition of 1914 as a Christmas gift in 1925.

7. *Diary*, 5 August 1921, Jonson Gallery archives.

12. New Mexico

1. Jonson talk to the Chili Club of Santa Fe, 29 August 1949.

2. *Diary*, 9 January 1923, Jonson Gallery archives.

3. Jonson to Reginald Fisher, 10 March 1956, Jonson letters.

4. *Diary*, 9 January 1923, Jonson Gallery archives.

5. *Diary*, n.d. (between 8 August and 2 September 1919), Jonson Gallery archives.

6. *Diary*, 9 January 1923, Jonson Gallery archives.

7. Jonson to Charles Morris, 11 January 1928, Jonson letters.

8. In *Raymond Jonson, A Retrospective Exhibition* (Albuquerque: University of New Mexico Press, 1964), in an interview with Van Deren Coke, there is this passage:

Q. Do you feel that your work continues consciously to reflect your environment?

A. I think some years ago I created my own environment and am still working in it. You might call it an inner environment if you like.

My works are really contrasts to the environment in which they exist. Around us we have realism, strife, pain, and greed. I wish to present the other side of life, namely the feeling of order, joy, and freedom.

13. Abstraction

1. *Diary*, 15 August 1920, Jonson Gallery archives.
2. Jonson to Charles Morris, 11 January 1928, Jonson letters.
3. Jonson talk to the Chili Club of Santa Fe, 29 August 1949.
4. Jonson to Ellen Van Volkenburg Browne, 6 May 1935, Jonson letters.
5. Jonson to Maurice Browne, 29 April 1935, Jonson letters.

14. Developments

1. Jonson to Charles Morris, 23 March 1928, Jonson letters.
2. *Diary*, 25 April 1922, Jonson Gallery archives.
3. Jonson to John Nichols, 19 May 1929, Jonson letters.
4. Jonson to Reginald Poland, 4 May 1938, Jonson letters.
5. Jonson to John Nichols, 1 April 1929, Jonson letters.

15. New York and Chicago

1. Jonson to his wife Vera, 11 October–23 November 1931.
2. Antonio Sant' Elia, *Manifesto of Future Architecture*, 1914.
3. Tom Vickerman, *Chicago Evening Post.* 12 January 1932.
4. Jonson to his brother Arthur, 16 June 1932, Jonson letters.
5. Jonson to his brother Arthur, 2 May 1937, Jonson letters.
6. Thomas Craven, *Men of Art* (New York, Simon and Schuster, 1936).
7. Jonson to his brother Arthur, 2 May 1937, Jonson letters.
8. Jonson to R. Vernon Hunter, n.d. [1934], Jonson letters.
9. There was, of course, a great deal more abstract work in the federal programs than Jonson thought. His opinion was based on the works he saw being installed under the program.

16. Trilogies and Cycles

1. On 28 August 1927, shortly after his arrival at the Grand Canyon, Jonson wrote to Vera, who had remained in Santa Fe:

It is immensely gorgeous—a hell of a hole in the ground full of detail and color—and infinite in variation. No one that I know of or anything I've seen expresses it at all. It is deep—high—concave—spacious—full of mystery and awesome. It is the strongest thing I have seen in nature. It is the most spiritual phenomenon of life I have seen—and it is inspiring.

2. There are three trilogies not in the Retrospective Collection. They are, *Sequence—a Trilogy* (1948) and *Kaleidoscopic Trio* (1957), both collection of Stewart Rose, Jr., and *Trilogy—The Square* (1962), collection of the artist.

3. C. J. Bulliet, "How Raymond Jonson Escaped Being Zoroaster," *Chicago Evening Post.* 19 January 1932.

17. The Spiritual in Art

1. Quoted in "Raymond Jonson Asserts Layman Can React to Non-Objective Painting," *Albuquerque Tribune*, 24 March 1938.
2. Jonson to Charles Morris, 28 July 1938, Jonson letters.
3. Jonson to Charles Morris, January 1938, Jonson letters.
4. Jonson talk to the Chili Club of Santa Fe, 16 December 1946.
5. Alfred North Whitehead, *Science and the Modern World* (New York: The Macmillan Company, 1925).

18. Absolute Art

1. Jonson to Charles Morris, 11 January 1928, Jonson letters.
2. Jonson to Reginald Fisher, 10 March 1956, Jonson letters.
3. Jonson talk to the Chili Club of Santa Fe, 29 August 1949.

19. Craftsmanship

1. *Diary* 3 July 1921, Jonson Gallery archives.
2. Jonson to Charles Morris, January 1938, Jonson letters.

20. The Airbrush

1. Harry Holtzman, who was familiar with the airbrush, suggested to Jonson that he try using it.
2. Jonson talk to the Chili Club of Santa Fe, 29 August 1949.

21. Color

1. Elaine de Kooning in *Art in America* 49, no. 4 (1961), wrote, "Pascin is reputed to have stepped off a train on a visit to New Mexico and have gotten back on again immediately, saying, 'This light is too bright for me.' It is certainly a light that consumes, a light to make moths of artists."
2. *Diary.* The entry, written at Peterborough in 1920, is undated.
3. Jonson talk to the Chili Club of Santa Fe, 29 August 1949.
4. "Raymond Jonson's Credo," New Mexico *Daily Examiner,* 31 December 1938.
5. Jonson to his brother Arthur, 2 May 1937, Jonson letters.
6. Jonson to his brother Arthur, 25 October 1937, Jonson letters.
7. Jonson-Garman tapes, 1956–1957.
8. Jonson to Reginald Fisher, 10 March 1956, Jonson letters.

22. Toward Fulfillment

1. Jonson to Reginald Fisher, 10 March 1956, Jonson letters.

23. The Artist's Materials

1. It was Henry W. Levison, an authority on the chemistry of artists' colors and head of Permanent Pigments, Inc., who developed and in 1957 made available under the trade name Liquitex the first complete, stabilized, and trustworthy acrylic polymer medium. Alfred Duca had invented polymer tempera in 1945, and other artists had been using synthetics for a number of years. Also in 1957 José Gutiérrez brought out his Politec brand in Mexico, but it must be said in honesty that Liquitex was a much more complete line, more versatile and reliable. Today, virtually all manufacturers of artists' colors produce lines of acrylic polymer paints.

Levison was, and continues to be, a scientific experimenter who has introduced many innovations and new colors. His great concern has been for the permanency of his product, one on which artists can confidently rely. One of the results of Jonson's adoption of the Liquitex medium has been a long-continuing and voluminous correspondence with Levison which explores all the facets of the medium and a consideration of the techniques involved in its use. So far as Jonson is concerned, he has often frankly stated that in his estimation the acrylic polymers constitute the greatest medium ever developed for artists.

24. Culmination

1. In a letter to Charles Morris on 11 January 1928, Jonson wrote, "It has not been my intention to make pictures of places and things but rather an effort to work out my own salvation."
2. Jonson to his brother Arthur, 23 April 1933, Jonson letters.
3. Jonson to his brother Arthur, 29 February 1932, Jonson letters.
4. Jonson to Eunice Tietjens, May 1919, Jonson letters.
5. Jonson to Doris Ogden, 22 June 1940, Jonson letters.
6. Jonson quoted in *Albuquerque Tribune*, 24 March 1938.
7. Jonson to Ed Garman, 6 November 1971, Jonson letters.

Index